APM Group

The **APM Group** is excited to sponsor *The Change Awards 2025.*

'It is not the strongest of the species that survives, nor the most intelligent, but the one most adaptable to change' is a famous quote based on Charles Darwin's work by Professor Leon Megginson.

APMG firmly believes in this principle and is committed to it. Our Change Management certification equips individuals, teams, and organizations with the essential tools to not only navigate the fast-paced changes of today's dynamic business landscape but to embrace and thrive in them. Change Management has become an essential skill for any leader to possess to meet both their personal and business goals.

We are delighted to be partnering with Tammy and Change Ninja to help formalize a qualification, launching later this year, to further support the development and recognition of this key skill within the workplace.

If you would like to be kept in touch with the development, then please scan the QR code below to join our mailing list.

Nicola Kelly, Product Innovation Director

I love this book. It's practical, accessible, and full of humour. So many innovative ways of addressing the problems life throws at you, I'll definitely be reaching for it next time I get stuck.

Jenny Landreth – Writer and script editor of all sorts of things, from episodic radio pieces and kids' TV animation to newspaper articles, reviews, and books

In this refreshingly jovial and light-hearted book about change, Tammy shares her own story of how she overcame a major personal challenge by using a suite of well-known change tools. These are tried and tested tools that are easy to apply and that can work wonders. If you're faced with a challenging situation in your personal life that you would like to change, look no further. Tammy's book is a great inspiration that will show how to do it.

Susanne Madsen – Author of *The Power of Project Leadership* and *How to do the Inner Work*

We have all been there: the life that had suddenly crashed, 3am panic wakeups, emotional turmoil, self-doubt, and seemingly no choices.

Tammy lets the reader into her home and psyche with the most actionable guide to change I have ever read. As all humans act irrationally, especially when exposed to adversity, we need a recipe for a way out when we feel stuck. Read this book to find your own recipe and awaken your hidden 'doer'.

Margo Waldorf – Founder at Change Awards

So much of this book resonates. It's a personal story and I was invested in the triumph of the heroine over adversity – yet it's not a tale of yore, battling against all odds, instead it's a practical and pragmatic approach and set of resources we can all use to deal with change. And that's why I loved it. It's to use when and however it is needed and I will be coming back to it time and time again.

Ian Clarkson – Director of Portfolio Management, QA Ltd

I was lucky to be invited to the Change Ninja Way retreat that accompanies this book. I realized within one of the first exercises Tam led, that I was holding on to an outdated narrative. I was projecting an experience of the past on to the present and it was inhibiting me from taking a necessary leap. Tam's supportive provocation, knowledge of how the brain works and the environment she created helped me to shift my perspective over the course of the weekend. If you want to release fears that's exactly what Tam's retreat (and book) is about.

Alex Barker – Co-author of *Be More Pirate*

Change is good they say… Close a door, a window opens. I know 'I should but…' Sometimes it doesn't feel good and we don't know where to start so how do I change 'Should' to 'Would'?

This book is not just an ordinary way to work through a change, personal transformation, or any day challenges in your life. Rather it's an EXTRAORDINARY way to support yourself!

This time it's personal, change ninjaing is a fantastic resource, manages all the above, creatively, skilfully, successfully.

Sam Brandes – Global Wellbeing Lead, Novartis

A story with purpose, humour, authenticity, and humanity that builds trust due to the author's vulnerability; tools that invite us, the reader, to dare to apply them to our own life situations encouraging us to be better at creating our own path. I was able to change my own neurobiology as I read it. This is a manual for being a human being.

Cath Cooney – Coach and Consultant

A poignant and personal journey that draws on the strength and resilience of the author in using change management skills, tools, and techniques to overcome personal challenges. Most of us do not have that strength and resilience, but we do now have access to the tools and techniques that she used to help us get through our own personal change to arrive at a happy ending.

Jooli Atkins – Digital Partnering NHS England

The world needs a new dynamic by which to engage, collaborate, innovate, and improve, we need to learn to adapt to more subtle and positive ways of engaging people in change, approaching change with more compassion and subtlety for healthier outcomes. This is what is at the heart of becoming a Change Ninja, and building on the awareness and insights from the first book, you can take away positive tools and methods to nimbly work around the challenges Tammy's book is a whole new dimension on dealing with people change and is leading the way in a space that is much in demand. Be the change and lead the way for yourself and others by joining the Change Ninja community!

Jo Stanford – CEO Healthcare Project and Change Association and Change Ninja!

Tammy's holistic approach to storytelling which guides you through the art of enacting change that makes a difference, has evolved, and informed my own ninja like practice. Her tools and top tips have enabled me to be brave, give things a go, and build in precious time to stop, reflect, and step forward with purpose and clarity for myself, my team, my organization, and my family.

Marie Hernandez – People Practitioner and Working Mum

In *The Change Ninja Returns*, Tammy masterfully intertwines her personal story with potent tools from the Change Ninja methodology, creating a transformative journey that resonated deeply with me. I was, quite literally, on the edge of my seat. With vulnerability and authenticity, Tammy invites us all to navigate the labyrinth of change, equipping us with incredibly useful practical strategies to tackle real-life situations head-on. I bloody loved it.

Michelle Minnikin, Captain of Culture at Work Pirates and author of *Good Girl Deprogramming*

the
Change
Ninja
RETURNS

Dare to Ninja

Tammy

And this time it's personal

Dr Tammy Watchorn

First published in Great Britain by Practical Inspiration Publishing, 2024

© Tammy Watchorn, 2024

The moral rights of the author have been asserted

ISBN   9781788606264 (hardback)
          9781788606271 (paperback)
          9781788606295 (epub)
          9781788606288 (mobi)

Every effort has been made to trace copyright holders and to obtain their permission for the use of copyright material. The publisher apologizes for any errors or omissions and would be grateful if notified of any corrections that should be incorporated in future reprints or editions of this book.

Want to bulk-buy copies of this book for your team and colleagues? We can customize the content and co-brand *The Change Ninja Returns* to suit your business's needs.

Please email info@practicalinspiration.com for more details.

For Chrumtree and Jac
With love

Contents

Foreword

Too many parts of our society are fundamentally broken. There are developed countries with people living in poverty. Wars, conflicts, and political instability are constant issues. Social inequality seems to be getting worse, not better. The combination of the energy crisis with the cost-of-living crisis is forcing some people to have to choose between heating and eating. Climate change is already affecting us with many concerned we have left it too late to deliver a meaningful response.

These problems are well known, but how do we get better at solving them? The United Nations has arguably led the way at a strategic global level through their publication of the *Sustainable Development Goals*, which they describe as a 'blueprint for peace and prosperity'. However, articulating the problem and knowing what needs to be done is not the same as actually putting the solutions in place. The hard reality is that fixing society's issues and delivering the 17 Sustainable Development Goals requires major coordinated change. And if there is a group of professionals that really understands how to deliver change effectively, it is project professionals.

Given the scale and complexity of these challenges, it is a tough time to be involved with delivering projects, programmes, or portfolios. This is where *The Change Ninja Returns* has the potential to create significant impact. It provides a broad range of tools and approaches for responding to the myriad of difficult situations that project professionals are likely to face. The practical and tactical advice in this book supports project professionals to transition from solving problems to effective strategy execution.

The other great advantage of '*being more ninja*' is that it can add value on both a personal and a professional level. Many of the strategies and concepts that are explored in this book for project delivery can also be used for life in general. Much like a complex project, life has a habit of throwing curve balls at us that need to be resolved. There is definitely something in here for everyone.

If nobody has said it to you today, let me take this opportunity to say thank you. Whether you are new to the project profession or have been with us for some time, your efforts are helping to address the world's toughest problems. Collectively, our profession is making the world a better place one project at a time.

And lastly, my thanks must also go to Dr Tammy Watchorn for introducing the world to the *Change Ninja* concept. At the heart of the project profession is the desire to deliver benefits for the public good and *The Change Ninja Returns* has pushed us further in the right direction.

I hope you enjoy reading this book as much as I did.

Prof Adam Boddison OBE
Chief Executive – Association for Project Management

Forward again!

You will have heard of the glass ceiling, the imaginary barrier at work that stops progression. But you will not have heard of the glass front door. The glass front door is the imaginary barrier at home that prevents useful ideas learnt in the workplace from being applied in the rest of your life.

In *The Change Ninja Returns*, Tammy has broken the glass front door. Once again, in a beautifully innovative, engaging gameplay book, Tammy has managed to take great ideas learnt for work and transport them into daily life. Just like her first book, *The Change Ninja*, this book is a steady progression of examples, laughter, and application.

Initially you will ignore the strap line, 'This time it's personal', assuming it's just a play on the words in the title but then slowly you will realize that it is personal – it is about real learning of useful ninja moves applied to real life challenges.

As you work along using the Performance Enhancement Tools (PETs) and score yourself on actions and decisions on the journey you will find your own barriers begin to dissolve. Written with open honesty the journey Tammy takes over the course of a year provides many insights into life and challenges which you will recognize from a first-person perspective.

Of course you may be wondering why I am not at all surprised by the rollercoaster of events and panoply of emotions that arise (hint – because I was there in the background) but when you have finished enjoying this book, no actually before you finish, get hold of *The Change Ninja* and in the name of work-life balance start ninjaing your life on the outside of your glass front door, at work, now.

Eddie Obeng
Burke Lodge Beaconsfield

Preface

Becoming a Change Ninja was never something I'd really thought about. I used to get up every day and drive into work where I would face battle after battle just to get the job done. At the time, the battles didn't stand out as battles, it was all just part of the role of 'delivering'. Dealing with the naysayers, the blockers, the 'that's not how we do things around here' brigade, and the big egos that always thought they knew better. It was all part of the system. It was the norm.

The norm until, that is, I decided there had to be a better way and I adapted my approach to leading change. Rather than trying to tackle things head on I instead started thinking about people over process, asking myself how I might best approach the individual 'blockers' to win them over, how I might get around the roadblocks using different tools, and how I might recruit volunteers to new projects in an unofficial way that didn't upset anyone's boss and allowed us to get things done under the radar.

Pretty quickly I realized that with small, stealth-like, Ninja moves I could deliver successful change quickly and effectively while bypassing the battles of old. People kept asking me how I did it and so I turned the stories into the *Change Ninja Handbook*, because I recognized that the battles I had faced were common battles for anyone leading change, irrelevant of position, grade, or organization. There was a real need, I thought, for more Change Ninjas and for those Ninjas to find a sense of belonging, to know that their issues were common to many people, and that there was a better way to do things.

And then a big, nay gigantic, life-changing event happened to me. One that shook up everything I knew and one that would require me to change my life and change how I lived. The difference this time was that there was a lot more emotion and a lot more riding on the outcome. It was a change where every decision would impact me directly. This time the battles weren't with other people but with myself, my own fears, thoughts, and doubts became the naysayers and blockers. My own self-imposed beliefs and norms became the 'that's not how we do things round here' brigade. This time the stakes were high, and any wrong move would impact me directly. There was no safety net. At all.

We all know that change can be challenging and when we can't really imagine a good outcome then change can also be terrifying. Fear, panic, anxiety, and doubts can take over and overwhelm us, making it difficult to make good logical decisions about what next, especially when we have no idea what the 'what next' could even be. Our ancient brains have evolved for survival and life-changing events can spell danger. When it's work related, we often have people to complain about; it's their fault, and never ours. When it's happening directly to you and only you can do something about it then it can feel a little different. Well, a lot different.

So, I asked myself, what would a Change Ninja do? And the answer, which seems obvious in hindsight but felt far from simple at the time, was to use all my Change Ninja skills, resources, and knowledge rather than trying to become more resilient in the face of adversity. Skills that I'd previously employed in the workplace to find ways around blockers that were (mostly) other people, I now used to find ways around the blockers my brain was creating. Rather than trying to tackle things head on, I instead used my resources to change the environment around me, thereby reducing the impact the stressors of the unwanted change had on me. When I felt like the lemons were pounding me in the face, I became determined that I would, somehow, make lemonade.

This is a story book, a real story, of how I used the resources available to me[1] to manage my way through an enormous, unwanted, life-changing event. Something I had no choice over but had to deal with anyway. It's a story where, in the face of adversity, instead of

---

[1] People, tools, skills, knowledge, and insights, many relating to my work.

trying to be super resilient and tackling things head on, I instead attempted to change my environment in order to remove, or minimize, the threats that were causing the anxiety and fear. It's a story where I became my very own case study, using all the tools I teach others to use for managing change in the workplace to see how well they would work when the change is unwelcome, scary, and anxiety inducing. Where every wrong move could lead to disaster.

This is also a story that acts as a guide to help you use your very own resources in different ways to manage some of *your* challenges in life. A story that shows that while you can't control what life throws at you, you can control, to some degree, your responses to what life throws at you. It's about controlling the story you tell yourself.

Chapter 1

Taking back control

I'd like you to think back to the last good bit of practical training you had at work. I don't mean the mandatory fire training course where you had to remember which specific extinguisher you needed for different types of fires.[1] I mean the kind of training that made sense, that would help you do your job better, that came with some practical tools to get things done more easily or in a better way. The kind of training that was about managing change better, managing time better, managing yourself more skilfully in the workplace. The learning might have been part of a formal course, or something you learnt from a book or an event perhaps. However you undertook the learning, it was something that resonated with you in such a way that you put the tools into practice once you were back at work.

Next, think about the last time you had a challenging situation at home. One that was impacting on

---

[1] Even though you have been told, under no circumstances, to never try and put a fire out at work – ever.

you personally, one that was emotionally challenging. Be honest, did you reach into your work toolkit for that trusted training or tool? Perhaps you did and it worked well. Or maybe you didn't because the challenge at home sent you into an emotional tailspin and the normal, composed, logical 'you' had departed the building.

It may seem obvious that many of the challenges you face at work are not dissimilar to the challenges you face outside work: other people doing things wrong; people not doing what you want; plans going squiffy; risks becoming issues; and feeling like it's one step forward and two back. But there is a significant key difference: you are much more emotionally involved in personal challenges because they impact directly on you and your life. And being more emotionally involved means the change can be much harder to manage, especially when it is uncertain, unexpected, and anxiety inducing because that emotion knocks the logic flying. When this happens, it can be all too easy to beat yourself up for being a failure or for imaging you are just not resilient enough, especially if those around you are telling you not to panic, that it will be fine, and that you just need to do 'XYZ' to sort it out. This is their way of trying to help and be supportive, but the reality is that it can often make you feel worse, because their advice is the advice they would give themselves, their reality is not your reality and being told it's easy to sort when it feels anything but just leads to increased feelings of personal failure.

But what if there was a way to manage yourself through the challenges life throws at you? What if you could become a Change Ninja, not just at work, but at life? What if, with a little insight and practice, you could put the skills, knowledge, and training you already have and use daily at work to help you do this? What if, instead of trying to be more resilient to the stresses you face, you could instead use these tools to change the environment around you and in doing so reduce the impact of the stressors, particularly if you are unable to influence or change the stressors them-selves?[2] What if you were able to use your resources to take control and tell your story the way you want to tell it? What if you could take those lemons and find a way to turn them into lemonade?

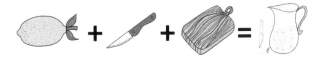

This book is both a story and a guide for how you, like me, can control your story and make lemonade.

---

[2] Imagine going to your favourite restaurant and they seat you under the loudspeaker when you just want a quiet night. You don't take on the waiter, arguing until they turn the music down, instead you politely ask to move seats. The speaker is still there, the music is still loud but by changing seats you've 'removed' the impact the music has on you, you can hear the conversation, the music becomes background rather than foreground. Rather than tackling the stress head on, instead you found a way to change *your* environment to remove or minimize the impact of something you had no control over.

This is how to Ninja your life

Author Note

Be warned. This is not, I repeat, not a typical empty calorie self-help book. By that I mean there are a gazillion books out there that tell inspiring stories of people down on their luck and walking through the desert for three months to 'find themselves'. These offer little by way of practical tools for everyday change and even if they are inspiring can make you feel a bit flat because you know that you couldn't do anything like this yourself. There are also a gazillion books out there with useful tools for day-to-day life management: journaling, doodling, yoga, time management, diet, sleep routines, and much much more. These tools can, and do, of course help, but these books can also leave you feeling a tad overwhelmed or feeling like a bit of a failure when, despite the promises you make to yourself, you seem incapable of using the tools on yourself regularly enough to have any real effect. You might talk about these books to others but often the reality is the actions you think you *should do* after reading them just become more things on your to-do list that you feel guilty about not doing.

For me, these books can be a bit like eating a family sized bag of Frazzles[3] at the end of a busy week. It feels good at the time but leaves you with a bacon flavoured

---

[3] Replace with a tasty but unhealthy snack of your choice.

hangover the next morning and a promise to yourself that you will never do that again. Until the next time.

And so, while this book is another 'self-help' book in many ways I'm hoping it's less 'empty calorie' and more like a superfood salad bowl that also happens to taste good and something you want to add to your weekly meal planner.

It's a book with a hopefully 'inspiring' story that demonstrates how to use a range of very practical tools for managing those, let's say, sub-optimal circumstances we face from time to time. Tools that put you centre stage, because really no one else, and I mean no one else, can change you. Only you can change yourself. If you practise the tools as you read the book, you will not only gain fresh insights for yourself, but will also associate the stories with the tools. And if you associate a story with a tool then when something similar happens to you in the future you are more likely to remember which tool to use because guess what? The story sounds familiar. Over time, with practice, you will know immediately which tool to use without needing the story. And that is when you realize you too are, in fact, Ninjaing life.

I want to offer a small caveat here: this is not a 'this will fix your life in an instant' book. Nor is it a science book, a clinical book, or an academic tome full of references.[4] The basic neuroscience I do reference is only

---

[4] Because who really has the time to go and check out all those references? There is, however, a list of additional reading options listed at the end of the book, should you wish to delve a bit more into the science.

here to act as a guide. A guide to help you notice how you feel, physically and emotionally, when faced with adversity, to help you understand why this change you are facing feels so awful. These feelings are a bit like your car warning lights, they signal that something isn't quite right and needs some investigation, that something is off and needs your attention.

If you are going through major trauma or have clinical mental health issues, then professional help may be needed. But if you are going through personal changes, big or small, or want to embark on a life change, then application of the tools in this book will help you get the outcome you seek.

Chapter 2

Why it stings when life throws you lemons

Can you remember a time in the past when something happened, and you had that feeling of dread in the pit of your stomach? Perhaps your heart rate increased? You felt panicky? Your mouth was dry? You felt sick? Or had a sense

of being totally overwhelmed? When the unexpected happens these physical feelings can be triggered and make you fearful of what's coming next. Even when the expected happens, these physical feelings can be triggered if it's not something you welcome. When you feel like this do you: hunker down and hide under the duvet?; try and pretend it isn't happening?; feel paralysed by the indecision of what to do next?; find your brain is unable to do anything *but* think about the thing that has happened? It can feel, in that fearful moment, that it might just be game over.

But fear not! Because with some basic neuroscience, a whole heap of noticing what is going on in your body (physical trauma) and your mind (emotions such as fear, anxiety, and panic), and a bag of useful tools, you can quickly learn to take back control over many grisly situations. And if you practice applying the tools in this book to your own life challenges as you read, you will soon find that you can shift yourself quickly from the *fearful* state to, if not a celebratory state, at least a place that feels a lot less scary.

Steps for dealing with fear

Step 1: It's not you, it's your subconscious brain

The fear state is not caused by a lack of resilience. The fear state results from your brain doing what it's designed to do; to keep you safe. The brain has evolved for your survival. Without you even being aware, the brain is constantly scanning the environment looking out for any changes, for things it doesn't recognize. Anything different could mean danger. Imagine a very hungry tiger has just jumped out in front of you. Your brain, without you even realizing it, will switch on the 'run' programme to try and get you away from the danger. You won't think about doing this, you will just do it. When faced with a potential deathly threat the brain switches *off* logical thinking (which is both energy intensive and relatively slow) and instead responds *emotionally* to the situation, in this case by giving you a boost of superhuman running abilities. You can run fast without even thinking because you are flooded with cortisol and adrenaline. It is this very same adrenaline and cortisol that triggers the stress/trauma response you physically feel when faced with an adverse situation.

Step 2: Emotion beats logic

Emotion on

Logic off

If your brain has decided it needs to switch your logic off and respond emotionally to get you out of danger, you can't use logic against it. If you don't believe me, remember the last time someone told you to calm down when you were angry. Did you do just that or did you yell back 'don't tell me to calm down!' while feeling even angrier. It's only on reflection that you accept calming down *was* the logical thing to do. Emotion beats logic. Every time. But if you notice that your emotions have taken over then you can, at least, try and work at getting your logic switched back on again.

Step 3: Knowing what's real and what isn't

Reality is the thing, out there in the world, that is solid. Your reality, however, is your perception of the thing out there in the world. Your reality is likely to differ from most other people's reality because your reality is created solely by you, in your brain and depends on many other factors. So, what feels very real to you is just your version of 'events'. It's also worth noting that reality doesn't care a jot about your thoughts and feelings and overthinking will not change it; only action can do that. Overthinking is, in most cases, just a way of procrastinating on action. But with the right tools, practice, *and* action you can change your reality to one that feels a little more palatable.

Step 4: Don't fight it but do notice it!

When deciding if something is safe or not your brain, at breakneck speed, processes all the data and information it has on file about the situation you find yourself in. It then predicts what might happen next. If it predicts a bad outcome it tells you to 'run' and you do (emotion is on/logic is off). If it predicts a good outcome then the logic stays on, and you start to get excited about this new opportunity.

You behave based on a 'prediction'. You think it's based on fact and reality but it's not. It's based on a prediction you aren't even aware you made!

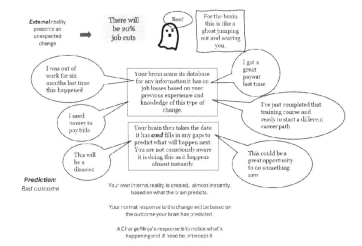

Step 5: A tiny bit of science can go a long way

If you notice your feelings (physical and emotional) and behaviours you can start to understand where they are coming from. If they are coming from a place of fear you can, with the right tools, start to challenge your brain's prediction and start to shift your thinking and response to the situation that doesn't feel too good.

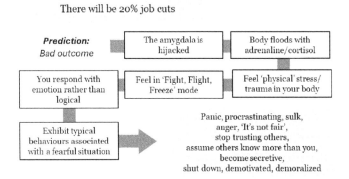

Vs

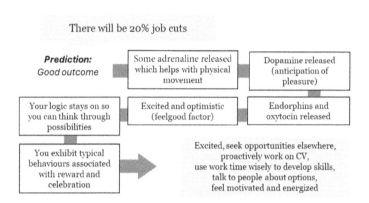

Step 6: Fear can be caused by a physical and social threat

A bullying boss, an angry neighbour, the 6 o'clock news, your car breaking down on the motorway, someone telling you 'yes, your bum does look big in that'. They can all induce the fear state, a bad outcome prediction.

Step 7: The brain can trick you into making the wrong decision

The brain likes the status quo over change because unless you've done the change before then it's more likely to predict a bad outcome. If you are in a bad situation, a job that's demotivating for example, then the brain might predict it's still better to stay than leave. That is because the status quo is familiar and therefore the brain knows what it's dealing with and can more accurately predict what will happen next, even if 'the next' isn't ideal for you. For the brain, and survival, the status quo can seem safer than an unknown. The brain can easily trick you into doing nothing even if doing nothing is not good for you.

Step 8: Stress isn't always bad

A stress response can, in fact, be good, because it can give you the energy and motivation to do something. You simply need to notice what is happening and use that flood of adrenaline surging through your body to propel you to move one step forward, to use it for action, however small that action is. Once you make that one step forward you will find you become motivated and energized to take another step forward.

Think about the nerves you feel in the pit of your stomach when you're about to give a presentation or do a parachute jump. Compare this to the nervous excitement (the feeling of butterflies in your stomach) when you're about to go on your third date with someone new or start a new job. Both are a result of adrenaline and the stress response, but you've possibly attached a story (emotion) of 'eeek' to the first feeling, and 'whoo-hoo' to the second. The first *feels* scary, the second *feels* exciting. The first you might be afraid to do, and the fear could stop you, the second you might be excited to do and the excitement motivates you into action.

These eight steps provide a basic view of what your brain is doing when faced with change, good and bad. Knowing this means you can start to notice the physical sensations you are feeling, and, when it's a fear response, try and do something about it. The emotion you feel, for example, sadness, anger, fear, is simply the story you've attached to the physical feeling. You can therefore try and change  the story, which will, in turn, change the emotions you feel, to excited and optimistic, for example.

If you were to break your leg, you wouldn't just give in to the pain and do nothing, you would get treatment. Similarly, if a warning light comes on in your car, you are unlikely to ignore it and will fix it or take it to the garage to find out what is wrong. The same logic applies to anxiety and panic. The stress response and physical feeling is a signal that something is wrong and needs treatment. But this time it's personal and it needs you to fix it, to find out the cause, to get the logical brain back in gear, to move forward one tiny step, to reframe the story and the emotional feeling, and to become unstuck. It sounds simple. It's not. But with practice you can start to manage it a little better.

So, remember kids… despite the curve balls life can throw at you (which are often beyond your control), you can, in many cases, choose how you respond to them, how you deal with them, how you tell your story and how you make decisions about what to do next.

Chapter 3

Climbing the stairs to make lemonade

This book is not simply a story book about change. Nor is it a book full of useful tools but possibly without context. It's a gamified book with a real call to action which, if you put in the work, will give you the tools for when life throws lemons at you. Your aim is to climb your way up the *STAIRs* and learn how to Change Ninja your life, how to make lemonade no matter how many lemons are pounding you in the face. Your ultimate challenge is to finish the book like a computer game, with three lives intact, a 100% health score, *and* a crate of lemonade.

So how will you do this?

First, I will give you my real-life story of a difficult situation and what I did to manage it. I will then guide you through an exercise using a Change Ninja tool of choice and invite you to apply the tool to a personal challenge you might have. These challenges might range from hugely exciting adventures, to difficult, emotional, rollercoaster life decisions. They may relate to home or work, but you will likely notice a bigger impact if you select emotionally charged challenges because the tools in this book are *particularly* useful for managing fear and panic inducing change. With practice, these tools *will* become life savers if you ever find yourself in survival mode, stuck, and needing to find a way out.

Each chapter has a section that uses the STAIR model.

1. The *story* of a challenging scenario is told.
2. The *tool* for managing this challenging scenario is then shared.
3. You then *apply* the tool to a personal challenge you might have just now.
4. You capture your *insights* about what you have discovered.
5. You *reflect* on how well the tool has worked and how you might use it in the future.

Each time you complete an exercise you will collect 'health points'. At the end of the book, you will add up the total number of health points you've collected and can convert these into: Lives; a Health Score; and Bottles of Lemonade.

If that sounds too 'easy-peasy-lemon-squeezy' then it is. Because this book is about challenging yourself and so I'm making it a little harder and you will be starting where I started. After the 'life changing event'. Where you're holding on with no lives, a very low health score, and zero bottles of lemonade.

So, are you ready to make lemonade? Then grab a notepad and pen and let's Ninja your life!

Chapter 4

Emergency help

What if you need particular help *right now* and don't have time to read the book? Fear not! Just follow this emergency guide for immediate help.

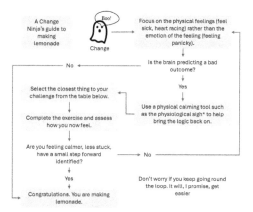

*The physiological sigh: Take two breaths in and one exhale. It feels a bit odd at first, but it quickly reduces CO_2 levels, slows down your heart rate, and leaves you feeling calmer, less tense, and more focused. It pretty much works instantly and is a great hack to have for those unexpected panic situations.

Ninja life move	Tool	Page
1. You have a change you need to manage but have no idea what to do, how to do it, or where to start. *You are stuck and need to get unstuck.*	Lost in the fog	48
2. You feel trapped between a rock and a hard place. A 'damned if you do and damned if you don't' scenario but you need to decide one way or the other. *You need to make a difficult decision.*	HardPlaceRock™	68
3. You feel totally overwhelmed with the sheer amount of things there are to do and you keep waking you up in the middle of the night remembering even more things you need to do. *You need to manage the feeling of being overwhelmed.*	StickySteps™	82

4. There are several options to choose from, but you absolutely want to make sure you make the right decision. *You need to see into the future.*	ISWON™	95
5. You're in a panic and can't think your way out of something that's happened. *You need fresh insights.*	MagicBoxOfTricks™	108
6. You're in a panic about particular situation that you probably can't do much about. *You need to distract yourself.*	SCARF	119
7. You need to do something but keep telling yourself you just can't do it because... *You need to stop making up excuses.*	Growth Mindset	136
8. You need to look at things from a different angle to make sure you don't make decisions on the wrong information. *You need to look at new perspectives.*	FiveEyes™	145

9. You need to learn from past activities to avoid making the same mistakes. *You need to stop beating yourself up.*	ActionReplay™	165
10. You need to control your story. *You need to tell a happy ever after.*	Story Telling	172
11. You are worried about all the things that might go wrong and need to find a way to get rid of the worry. *You need to banish the risks.*	Fix-It-Now™	182
12. You have some ideas of how you want to change your behaviours, actions, or thoughts. *You need to form some new habits.*	Habitz™	199

Chapter 5

Characters

You

You are resilient, tenacious, have dreams and goals that you work towards, you stick to your plans but can also take acceptable (to you) risks. Things might not always go according to your plan but when that happens you brush yourself down, accept it, learn from it, and start again. You are what you describe as realistically optimistic. Others might think you have confidence and courage because you just seem to get on with things and very little shakes you. You laughingly call this your Batfink Wings.[5] But of course, you are also human. And just like everyone else, you can suffer from imposter syndrome. You can feel left out, lonely, at odds with others, imagine *everyone* else is doing better at life than you, and you sometimes just want to hide under the duvet. You just don't let on, at least to most people, and sometimes not even to yourself. Because acknowledging and showing that you sometimes feel scared and vulnerable is, well, a hard and scary place to go.

---

[5] Batfink is a cartoon character from the 1980s whose famous phrase was 'bullets cannot harm me, for my wings are like a shield of steel'.

But here's the thing.

We all have a breaking point when we can no longer do the pretending thing, when pretending would be harmful. And that point is different for us all. What may seem like a simple change for one person can easily send another person into a tailspin. The challenge is recognizing and accepting this and knowing that just because something is easy for someone else, doesn't mean it's easy for you. If you are able to recognize when you are in a bit of a tailspin, then you might also remember that instead of beating yourself up for not being resilient enough you should instead focus on changing the environment you find yourself in using the resources you have available. Trying to tough it out and tackle the stressors head on is probably the worst thing you could do, especially if they are beyond your control. Changing the environment you find yourself in may not remove the stressors, but it will make them just a little bit less stressy.[6]

You are determined, once and for all, to learn how to use your resources, tools, network, capabilities, and skills effectively to Ninja your life.

---

[6] Imagine you are having the same fight yet again with your partner. You know shouting is going to make you feel worse in the longer term and not resolve anything. Perhaps instead you could leave the room and compose a text once you are calm that explains why you are so upset, or suggest you talk about it calmly the following day. The thing you are arguing about might still be there, but you can deal with it in a different way if you use your tools effectively. In that way, you can change the 'in-the-moment' angry environment of the argument to a more conducive calm conversation. This will make you feel a lot better overall and you are more likely to find a resolution that works for you both.

Exercise

Make a quick note of all your skills, capabilities, qualities, and tools that might be useful for managing change on page 30. These can be anything from leadership, management, communication, risk tools, presentation skills, tools you use for creative thinking or designing webpages or managing budgets. Think of it as your personal CV of stuff you do well. Don't be shy. No one is looking. Now congratulate yourself on having such a good personal CV of stuff you do well. You rock!

Dementors[7]

These can be family, friends, or colleagues. They might be the types of people who as soon as you mention something, like 'I'm going to Barcelona', instead of saying 'oh how lovely', or 'how long for?' or anything that shows an actual interest, instead

---

[7] Stolen shamelessly from the Harry Potter books. Dementors literally suck the life out of you, leaving you an empty withering shell barely able to function. Your real-life dementors might not be *this* bad but when you're on a 'shuggly peg' and could easily crash and burn, do you really want to take the risk of being made to feel like you don't count? Or made to feel like it's all your fault? Or made to feel like you are somehow 'lacking' and will never succeed?

will say 'we went there ten years ago, and you should go to this restaurant because it's really good'. Or when you tell them you are struggling at work, instead of asking you what's going on, or how could they help they instead tell you how they managed to get a new job three years ago and you should just do what they did. Or perhaps you've just won the lottery to get into the London marathon and when you share the news instead of saying 'well done you, how exciting for you', they say things like 'well that wouldn't be my idea of fun but if it that's what you want to do then… .'

They are easy to spot because they quickly bring the conversation back to themselves, telling you what they would do or what their opinion is.

This doesn't mean they are bad people, or people you shouldn't have as friends (if they're family though you probably have no choice!). They could be incredibly good fun, they could be good running pals, or pals you go to the cinema with because they like the same types of films. But they are not, I repeat, not, the type of people you need to engage with when you are feeling utterly overwhelmed, panicky, or anxious. They will not make you feel any better and may even make you feel worse. And while they are likely to give you advice, whether you ask for it or not, it's unlikely it will be useful advice. The best thing to do with these people is to stay in touch, meet them only if it suits you, never share too much, and never ask them for advice if you have any inkling that it's not going to give you what you need. Even on those nights when you feel lost, lonely, panicky, wanting the right company and decide to 'WhatsApp' everyone, do yourself a favour and miss out the dementors. They won't make you feel better. Ever. You know it, I know it. But only you can break that cycle.

Exercise

Make a quick note of who these people might be on page 30. You might also want to write down the reason they are people you do want in your life normally, but why they aren't the right people to help with emotional change.

Wing people

These are people who 'have your back'. They love you regardless. They listen, empathize, coach you if you have things to work through, ask how they can help and what you need, and always find time for you despite being busy with their own life and issues. They are the people who, when something good happens, find joy in your joy.[8] These might be family, old friends, or colleagues. Each one may have something specific to offer so use them wisely and spread the load. Decide how they can help and go to them for that help. You don't want to overburden them, but you'll know, instinctively, who they are. If there is any doubt, you can check they're not really dementors using the 'three strikes and you're out' rule. They don't have to be very close friends; they just have to provide a particular thing you might need.

Exercise

Make a note of all these lovely people you know on page 30. Write down qualities or skills they might possess that might help your current situation.

---

8 Freudenfreude. This means they find joy in your joy and are genuinely happy for you even if they have a lot of bad stuff going on in their own life. It's the opposite of schadenfreude, where people take delight in your misfortune. You secretly suspect some of your dementors have schadenfreude.

'Wing people' in the making

Be open to new connections in unexpected areas[9] and you may be pleasantly surprised with what you find. We're all looking for human connection. You just need to find one 'hook', one connection, one thing in common with someone and, *et voilà*, you have another person with whom to connect with and share certain aspects of your life.

You may have met this person randomly, almost in passing, and realize that they could be a wonderful addition to your 'bag' of good people. Don't be afraid to ask if you can exchange numbers. They're probably thinking the same but are just too shy to ask.

Exercise

Make a note on page 30 of anyone new in your life who you think could be a good wing person; commit to developing the relationship with them.

---

[9] While out walking the dog, at an online seminar, on X (formerly Twitter), in the local cafe. Places you wouldn't 'normally' look to meet new 'wing people'.

Of course, it could be entirely possible that you have people who are both dementors *and* wing people at the same time. This depends entirely on what it is you are looking for in them and what they can offer that will support you in your hour of need. For example, someone might be a terrible coach when you are looking for fresh insights, but they may be able to provide excellent knowledge and advice about something more tangible, such as financial matters.

Cut-out-and-keep wing person

For an actual 'cut-out-and-keep wing person' please head to the back of the book.

Your skills, qualities, capabilities, and tools	

Dementors – avoid	

Wing people – use wisely	Qualities and skills

Wing people in the making	Qualities and skills

Chapter 6

A call to action

A s my story begins, I invite you to time travel back with me and read alongside as it happened, in real time. I invite you to feel and relate to my emotions of pain, panic, and sometimes joy, before applying the tools I used for each different scenario to your own personal challenge(s).

Chapter 7

Dream a little dream

It's the 3rd January. I've just packed away the remnants of Christmas and New Year. Christmas was fairly typical. We had my partner's family over, the usual Christmas dinner was followed by the usual move to the lounge, where the TV was on too loud and everyone shouted over each other, and the TV, until it was time for more food, and everyone descended on the leftovers. I had spent much of the time tuned out and daydreaming, occasionally nodding my head and shouting 'really?' when I knew I was supposed to be surprised at something or laughing along at the appropriate moments. The stories told were the stories that always got told and I knew them a little too well.

I sit down with a fresh coffee and recall what I was daydreaming about just over a week ago. Although I could barely hear myself think over the din of

Paddington taking on Hugh Grant while the family stories bounced around, I had started to imagine how nice it would be to have some of the calm back that I'd relished during that weird lockdown period. A period when, despite the horror and uncertainty that a pandemic brought, also gave me, possibly for the first time in years an inner 'quiet', something that I now realize I am desperately craving.

As I sip my coffee, I reflect on my life just now. I know it's a pretty good life and I have absolutely no reason to complain *but* I do have a rumbling of dissatisfaction, a slight feeling of unease, and I know I've had this for a while. It's the feeling that I could quite easily keep doing what I'm doing, in this perfectly nice life, for the next 20 years or so only to find that they pass in a flash leaving me wondering where they have gone. I want – I decide as I finish my coffee – peace, calm, and adventure. I accept, as I rinse out the coffee mug,[10] that calm and adventure aren't necessarily compatible but I'm creative and pretty sure I know what I need to do. It's time, I think, to take a wee[11] bit of a risk, and maybe make one of those dreams my partner and I have often talked about actually happen. We are a long-term couple, almost 30 years, and like every relationship we have had our ups and downs, but we are still here. And

---

[10] This story is real, and I've tried to be as accurate as possible but there are some fabrications for effect. Rinsing out my coffee cup after I've finished is a pure fabrication. The reality is more likely that I left it on the table despite heading to the kitchen straight after!

[11] Wee is Scottish for small. Smaller than small really, minuscule almost.

while the last couple of years have not been the easiest for us, with more downs than ups, we do still have the same shared dreams of our future. Perhaps, I think, as I put the clean and dried cup away[12] a wee adventure will do us both a world of good. An adventure will, I think, give us something positive to focus on while we continue to get past some of our more recent issues, possibly even, I think, perhaps getting a little carried away, turn us back into being the best version of us.

I grab the dog's lead and my jacket and head out for a walk and some more thinking. I know I will need to present my thinking to my partner in a way that will not scare him too much as he really doesn't like change. As I walk, I start to picture a move to the country: a cottage; chickens; goats; slower pace of life; waking up to great views; spending weekends in the hills and lochs. It would be a project we could do together, as a couple, something we perhaps haven't been the best at doing in the last couple of years, both having morphed into quite different social circles. And it could be a way for my partner to retire early, or at least have the option to if we were able to 'downsize' a little. This I think smugly, is the killer selling point.

---

[12] Erm…, see previous footnote. This is definitely fiction, delusional even!

As we sit down to dinner that night, I explain my thinking about us moving to the country, away from the city, and list all the good reasons why. Surprisingly he is pretty receptive, excited almost, and what follows is a pretty good chat about what we both might want out of such a move. We also share some of the worries it might also bring because for us, it's a pretty big life-style change. The more we talk, the more excited we both become and the more it feels like this could actually be something we don't just talk about doing but might just actually do.

As he cleans up the dinner plates, I smile at how easy a sell this seemed to be but also know that I need to prepare myself for what will inevitably follow once things are put in motion. The excitement for him will, I know, wear off as the anxiety and nerves of change kick in. But I'm ready for this move, despite my own nerves, and will try and manage his doubts so that they don't impact on me too much and cause me to change my mind. This means I will take on the role of excited optimist while he is the anxious pessimist, but this is nothing new. These are the roles we have played out time and time again for pretty much any type of change in life, however big or small the change has been. This time I'm ready for it.

Once the dishes are done and we are sitting comfortably on the sofa we open up a property search engine and start to see what is out there, what possibilities there are. It feels incredibly exciting.

The next day I engage a solicitor to start the selling process. Even though we aren't quite ready to put our house on the market yet, we agree it would be a good idea to be ready to press go quickly if we see something we like. We will, I know, need to be in a position to move fast.

I agree a time with the solicitors for someone to pop round and get the paperwork initiated. I have that nervous excited churn in my tummy that change often triggers. I can't decide how much is nervous nerves versus excitement, but I decide to keep my feelings to myself because even though no concrete decisions have been made, my partner has already started to do the 'what if' panicking for the both of us. I teach and train others in the neuroscience of change management and know that this slight churning feeling I have is normal and that my mindset can, to some degree, control the emotional feeling that goes with it (excited or scared). I am excited, I tell myself, this is a good thing. But I also accept that I've lived in the city my entire adult life, lived in the same house for 20 years, one I painstakingly remodelled, and so my life just now feels safe and comfortable and I'm about to change all that for an unknown. I know this comfort and safety is part of why I want the change and that I'm making a choice to move but I can't know for certain that it will work out. I can't really imagine what the reality of it will be like because I have nothing to base it on. No previous experience to indicate that it will be OK. No data the brain can draw on to tell it this is a good move. And so, my brain, in trying to protect me from potential harm, is casting all manner of 'what if' questions and doubts. What if I hate it, what if he hates it, what if it makes our relationship harder, what if I feel trapped and isolated? But I know that it's normal to feel nervous and doubtful about change, even one I've instigated and want. My focus, I remind myself, is to try and tell positive stories rather than 'what if' stories. This will help me feel less 'eeek' and more 'hurrah'. I pay close attention to how my body is physically feeling because I also know that the nervous churn is caused by a flood of adrenaline triggered by the brain if it thinks there is potential danger. By noticing this physical feeling, I can quickly intercept it by telling me, my partner, anyone, about our plans and how exciting they are. The more I tell the story this way, the more my brain starts to recognize the future story as a positive one, and instead of filling the data gaps with 'eeek' it fills them with 'hurrah'. It starts to see the change will be the good and rewarding kind. It doesn't totally switch of the adrenaline flood, but instead of using the adrenaline to run away from the change, it instead uses it to motivate and move me towards our goal.

It's Friday morning a few weeks later and I'm feeling a bit glum as I haven't seen anything on the property market that would be a good match for us. All of the positive story telling has really got me ready to do this move and once I'm decided on things, I get very impatient about them. But it's starting to feel like it might have just been a dream after all as I had hoped we would have visited a few places by now. I decide to do one last search with a slightly different filter before promising myself to give it up for the day and focus on doing something more productive.

And there it is. The dream house. Perfect size, in a village with an active community, surrounded by wooded hills and overlooking a beautiful loch. It even has a mini annex for the ageing in-law should he wish to live with us at some point. I call the agents immediately and plan to visit the next day.

We visit, fall in love with the house, do all the relevant schmoozing with the seller, and on Monday morning we put in an offer. This is Scotland where houses are typically purchased in a blind auction. I have all my fingers and toes crossed. Do I have any reservations?

Absolutely. But I'm a Change Ninja and I need to practise what I preach, embrace the fear, and seize the opportunities. I think we can do this.

Chapter 8

Into the abyss

It's Wednesday morning and a typical cold, bleak, grey February day but I'm hopping up and down with excitement because today we find out if the offer we have made on our dream house in the country has been accepted. My body is physically buzzing from the cocktail of hormones and neurotransmitters caused by this potential change ahead of me and I'm bouncing off the walls. I'm full of 'what if' doubts of panic (with the associated feeling of churning tummy and heart racing caused by the adrenaline) while simultaneously excitedly planning where I'll put the furniture (with the associated overly excited feeling caused by dopamine). If our offer is accepted, then our lives will be significantly different from now on, and even though I want this move I still really can't imagine what it will be like.[13] The morning goes by incredibly slowly and I can't concentrate on anything other than clock watching, waiting for noon, the time at which the blind auction ends and the winning bid is revealed. 'Why is this taking so long?' I think for the umpteenth time as the clock hand moves to ten minutes past twelve. And then the phone rings, my solicitor's name flashes up. I answer it immediately, holding my breath in anticipation only to hear the words 'sorry but they went with another offer that was lower than yours. The buyers had already sold their house so had the cash for a quick sale'. The dopamine slumps, and I get a huge physical crashing feeling of disappointment.

I desperately ask if going back with an even higher bid could work but know that the system doesn't support this approach. The solicitor advises, not for the first time, that we really should sell our house first, get the money in the bank and then be in a position to make a quick sale on any future property. It's not a position I'm comfortable with as I really want to end up with the right house and not feel rushed into a purchase because we have nowhere to live.

I let them know that we'll think about it, thank them, and put the phone down, hugely disappointed. My feelings have gone from nervous and excited to deflated and low in a matter of seconds and my energy

---

[13] It's hard to imagine how something brand new might actually *feel*. But it's really easy to imagine things going wrong and how much a disaster it would all be.

levels – the ones that had me bouncing off the walls just twenty minutes before – have flatlined.

I decide not to call my partner straight away as I suspect he might be relieved because the more real this has become the more his nerves have been jangled and his relief will make me feel even worse. As I head downstairs to make some tea and think about a possible lunch, I hear the dog bark and the clatter of the letter box. I pick up the mail and find it's mostly the usual rubbish about random cheap deals in the middle of supermarkets but notice, nestled amongst all the rubbish, a white envelope addressed to my partner. A foreboding feel comes over me. For no reason at all I remember a time last year when I accidently found something out. Something that caused me to question our relationship. Something that I thought was firmly in the past and dealt with. For no reason at all I have the same 'pit of the stomach' feeling of dread I had back then, and I don't really understand why. I look at the envelope again. There is no indication at all of what it contains so I know I'm probably being silly but still, I decide to open it.[14] I very quickly discover that my gut feeling was right.[15] I feel utterly, utterly winded. I feel sick. In that split second, in opening that envelope, I realize that the life I have, the life I know, is over, done,

---

[14] Yeah, yeah, I know this is supposedly illegal but sometimes needs must.

[15] It mostly is. Ignore your gut feeling at peril. The gut, often referred to as the second brain, often knows things before you do, or at least your conscious you. Real Change Ninjas have learnt to trust their gut feelings.

gone forever. I acknowledge that there will be no going back and no fixing this time. I realize with absolute heart-breaking clarity that I will need to be strong, and I will need to call it a day and leave my partner. The relationship is over. Done. Finito. And it's me who is going to have to be brave and make that decision for the both of us, a decision based on their actions and their very poor judgement.[16] In less than ten minutes I've gone from planning an exciting new life in a dream home and location with my long-term partner to being thrown into an absolute and utter uncertain future life, alone. This is, I realize in that instant, a life-changing event I never imagined. Ever. And I have no idea what to do.

My life score plummets to 0, my health score is reduced to a paltry 20 and that crate of lemonade – the icing on the cake of country living with my partner and chickens – is gone. Gone in the opening of a plain, white, unmarked envelope.

Life score 0

Health score 20

Lemonade bottles 0

<u>Health points = 20</u>

---

[16] I know you're curious. But the content of the envelope matters not a jot to the story or anyone outside of the story. You just need to know it was big enough and bad enough for me to have to walk away. To walk away from my life, as I knew it.

What next?

In less than ten minutes I've gone from bouncing off the walls with nerves, anticipation, and excitement about buying a lovely house in the country to realizing my lifetime of 'normal' no longer exists. The home I created is now just bricks and mortar. The dreams I had for our future together no longer make sense. Where do you go when your whole adult life as you know it has been pulled from under your feet? How do you react and what do you do next? I could, I think to myself, just crumple, and give into the overwhelming gut-wrenching feelings I'm feeling. I could, I think, pretend I haven't opened the envelope, but know that I can't unknow what I've found out. I could get angry even though weirdly I don't feel any anger at this point.

A very small part of me, however, recognizes that what I'm physically feeling is stress and trauma. That the emotions I'm having are linked to my brain jumping into survival mode. I recognize that I need to, now more than ever, not give in to the emotion and try and keep my logic switched on so I can do the right things – for *me*. While this is far from easy, it is essential. I know that if I give in to the emotion of it all I may well make some bad choices. I may say things I don't want to say. I may be talked out of my decision to end the relationship which deep down I know will only prolong the pain, it would be a sticking plaster on a bad situation at best. I need logic and calm. There will, I know, be time for tears and anger later. And so, I pause, do some calming breathing,[17] take stock and have a word with myself. I'm smart and can be fiercely independent when I need to be. I've built my own successful business teaching, coaching, and mentoring others in how to manage change in a positive way. I'm even writing a handbook on how to be a Change Ninja.[18] Would there ever be a better time to test out what I teach on my own unasked for and scary life change? All of these tools for leading change at work, for managing the emotions of change, how would they work on my very own change? What if I tried to approach this unexpected change in the same way I might approach a project my theoretical boss might throw at me on a grey February afternoon? This is a typical 'foggy' project I think; it's a type of change where I don't know what to do and don't know how to do it, but I do know I can't stay where I am. Just like being caught in the fog on a mountain top. I also know that a foggy project requires baby steps. Teeny tiny toatie[19] wee steps, before assessing at each teeny tiny toatie wee step what has changed and what new

---

[17] The physiological sigh: Two breaths in and one exhale. Repeat 4–5 times for instant success.

[18] Shameless plug. Sorry, not sorry.

[19] More Scottish and meaning incredibly small.

information is now available before making a decision about the next teeny tiny toatie wee step.

The gut-wrenching emotions start to subside a little as I think this through. I still feel sick, full of fear and panic, but importantly I'm still thinking logically and haven't let the emotion of the situation overwhelm me. This is far from easy, but I know it's essential for me at this point to stop me giving in to all of the grief, fear, and panic which will not only make me feel worse but may end up with me not having the courage to do what I know I have to do. I've managed to distract myself by putting myself in the third person to work out what's going on and what I need to do next. I take the first teeny tiny toatie wee step forward out of this fog, pick up the phone and call my soon to be 'ex' partner. He is, I know at this point, totally unaware of what has happened in the last 30 minutes.

I then do the hardest thing I've ever had to do. Not exactly from choice but there was no other choice. I end the relationship. Done. Dusted. Non-recoverable.

He drives back from work, we agree he will move out while we sort things out, and he packs a bag and leaves. This bit is easier than I had imagined but he knew what he had done and so I suspect he was expecting this at some point. Once he's left, I try to focus on what my next tiny step out of the fog might be rather than collapsing into the grief of it all. It's far too soon to expect the fog to lift but taking small steps in hopefully the right direction will, I know, give me the motivation I need to keep going. There will be time for wallowing later. I also know that I shouldn't make any big, especially if they are non-reversible, decisions about my future that I might later regret, because I don't yet have any idea about what I want my future to look like. What, I wonder, will be an easy thing to do that will distract me from thinking about how awful I feel and will stop me feeling like I'm stuck and not knowing where to go next?

The perfect task presents itself. Perfect because it needs doing. Perfect because it will definitely make me feel better and, irrelevant of what happens next, will feel like I've done something useful.

I decide to have a clear out. You know the ones where you empty out all the cupboards and create a big, huge mess in the middle of the room before deciding what to keep. Clearing out, I know, is really good for the soul.[20]

---

[20] There is a lot of research suggesting decluttering can make you feel as if a weight has been lifted. It allows you to cross things off the to-do list, which gives you a sense of accomplishment *and* a sense of a fresh start and freedom. Getting organized also promotes greater productivity, a sense of order, and feelings of self-efficacy, as well as improving your mood. It's a good thing to do in a crisis.

Life ninja move 1

Story: Think of a change in your life right now. Do you?

a) Know what you are trying to achieve (clear goal) or not?
b) Know how to do the change (you've done something very similar before) or not?

There are four types of change, depending on your answers, and each requires a different approach.[21]

You probably manage a lot of change automatically, if you have a clear goal and have done it before, like going on holiday for a week to the same place every year.

It has a clear goal, and you know exactly what to do without thinking about it. You just need to work through your to-do list.

But what about that dream of living in the country that comes with chickens and sheep? The goal is clear, but you've never looked after chickens and sheep before. It's something you may need to learn about as you go. For this type of change you need more than just a checklist of actions because until you learn some new things you don't know what your to-do list will be.

---

[21] More examples can be found in *The Change Ninja Handbook* or in Professor Eddie Obeng's *All Change!*

Then there is change you have to do even if you don't really want to, like me ending my relationship, or you leaving that terrible job you have. Change where you have *no* idea what your end goal is and *no* idea how to do it (because you've never done this before) but *do* know that you need to do something because it's unsafe to stay where you are. This type of change can be difficult to initiate because the brain, in trying to protect you, might tell you that staying put is the safer option. Staying put is familiar and the brain can 'predict', with greater accuracy, what will happen next. It might tell you that yes you have a bullying boss, but you also have a wage, and it predicts that the wage is the safe option despite the bullying boss. With this type of change your brain might be telling you it would be safer to do nothing, but your gut might be telling you otherwise, that you need to leave this job despite not having a new job to go to, yet. This type of change can create so much anxiety that you might just feel well and truly stuck and have no idea what to do for the best, just like being lost in the fog.

Tool: When you are in the fog it's easy to get stuck. It's easy to procrastinate because the change feels too over-whelming and scary. And that is why you need to take teeny tiny toatie wee steps to inch yourself forward, learning and gaining insights as you go, until the fog begins to lift. Only once the fog has lifted and you have a clearer idea of the end goal should you make any life-changing decisions. The first step you take doesn't even need to be in relation to the big change at all. It just needs to be a step. A step that moves you from one place to the next. It will distract from the terrifying thing and that will help reduce your emotional fight/flight/freeze reaction and help switch your logical brain back on. While doing the action on this first step your brain will also subconsciously mull things over logically, working out what's best for you in the background. And once you have done the action you will get a feeling of achievement because, despite the situation you are in, you will have done something positive, and this will activate the reward part of your brain, which in turn will make you feel good, and so you will be motivated to take another step forward.

 Application: Think of something you are procrastinating on just now. It doesn't need to be a huge life changing decision thing but something chunky enough that's making you feel like you are stuck. Something that's playing on your mind every time you remember you haven't yet started it. Something that's making you beat yourself up for repeatedly not doing, perhaps telling yourself you're lazy, or useless, or that it's just too hard.[22]

Now think of a very small task you could do that might feel like you've at least made a start in relation to

---

[22] Like me editing this book!

the change. Make it a small and achievable action,[23] nothing that requires any big decisions. If you are thinking of leaving your job, for example, then the action might be in relation to researching other organizations, checking out LinkedIn profiles for ideas on how to spruce up your CV or talking to people in other departments about opportunities. A small achievable action that will give you more direction or information and will nudge you forward enough to get you unstuck.

Write your small manageable task here:

_____

_____

_____

Insights: What is the action? Can you do it just now? Like arrange a meeting with someone. If not, can you put time in your diary to do it later? Can you commit, right now, to when you will do the very small first step forward thing? Just putting it in your diary is, after all, an action, it's a teeny tiny toatie wee

---

[23] Like me telling myself I just need to edit this chapter today.

step and it means you have made a start to getting
unstuck.

How do you now feel now? Take a few minutes to
notice your physical and emotional feelings? Is there
a shift? A small sense of relief perhaps, or an ounce of
motivation to at least do the first step?

 Reflection: Being lost in the fog of
change is no different to being lost in the
actual fog on a mountainside. If you want
to find your way to safety get off a foggy
mountain the last thing you want to do is stride off
confidently in any direction because you might end up
striding off the cliff. Instead, you would take a small
step and reassess where you are and where to go next,
inching yourself out of danger until you can see a clear
path to safety.

Significant change, especially life changes that are
emotional, can be really hard to make because you
can't always imagine a good outcome and might not
know what to do because you've never done it before.
Remember this is because the brain, in trying to protect
you, has made some predictions about the change, the
more uncertain the change is, the more likely your
brain will suggest it's a change to be avoided. And so
you get stuck and procrastinate because it seems easier
and safer to not do anything. This is not because you
lack resilience or are weak, it is because your body is
undergoing a physical trauma response, a response to
which you've attached the emotions of anxiety, fear,

and panic. Doing nothing is like a 'freeze' response, and can be a way of trying to ignore the change rather than dealing with it. It's hunkering down on the mountainside hoping the fog will lift.

But once you start to break things down into small manageable chunks it's much easier to face the fear and make a start. You only need one small action, one tiny step to move you forward and get unstuck.

Each tiny step you take will remove a little bit more of the fear. Each tiny step will give you better clarity and will make you feel like you are progressing things even if you still aren't sure what the end point will look like. Each step you take will give you the energy and motivation to take the next step and eventually the fog will start to lift.

Points time: If you captured a small actionable step you can do then gain 30 health points.

If you have committed to doing the step (for example, put it in your diary) or took a break from the book to go and do it then gain an additional 20 health points.

Deduct 10 health points if you do nothing. This book is all about you and your life changes which is a call to action. Doing nothing will result in just that. Nothing.

Health points = _____

A week later and I've cleared out all the cupboards in the house and got rid of years of collected rubbish. I've put things into various piles: a pile of the ex-partners stuff for him to collect, a pile for the charity shop, a pile for recycling, and a pile for the skip. The skip pile is larger than it should be and it makes me feel guilty about the waste. I don't even like shopping, so I'm flummoxed at the amount of rubbish that has built up.

I've also been pretty ruthless, trying to not keep things as a 'just in case'. How much do we hold onto 'just in case', even though we can't remember the last time we used it? I recognize that, like most people, I make excuses and hold onto things that no longer serve me well.[24] The brain, I remind myself, really quite likes the status quo as it feels safe. Even if the status quo isn't safe, moving into an unknown space can seem to the subconscious brain riskier than staying put. And if we do this for relatively minor decisions, like keeping that coat 'just in case', then

---

[24] Is it too soon to say, 'for example long-term partners that are probably no longer good for us'? Probably yes, so I'll not say it. Just yet.

how likely are we to also do it for enormous life changing decisions?[25] It makes me realize just how much I have, in the past, procrastinated on making decisions because it's just so much easier, and seemingly less risky, than making the decision to do something and then having to act on the decision while not being 100% sure that the outcome might be a good one.

This very small, tiny step of clearing out some cluttered cupboards has given me much more clarity on the next step. Because it has distracted me, just for a brief amount of time, from the fear and pain of the situation. And by focusing on an activity rather than the trauma of what has just happened I feel a lot calmer than I might have done. And I actually feel quite good. Doing things that need doing, ticking things off a list, is, I know, all part of the brain's reward centre and so I get the accompanying feel-good factor from the dopamine that it has induced.

So, what is this clarity? What is my next step?

I have decided I need to rip the sticking plaster off and stick with the original plan. I need to continue with my dream of moving to the country and having an adventure, even if it's not quite the adventure I originally had in mind. I need to sell the marital home and start again, somewhere else.

---

[25] Still too soon to mention 'the ex'?

Chapter 9

Between a rock and a hard place

Once I've made the decision to continue with my dream, I do feel a little better, only 0.01% better but it's better than nothing. I'm still not really feeling much anger, mostly just grief, but this does feel like I'm taking back some control over the situation I'm in. It feels less reactionary and more proactive. I shouldn't let anyone, I think, stop me having my dreams. The fear of my 'what next?' and the hurt of what has happened is still incredibly raw, but I do know that by doing these small steps the fog has started to clear a little. I also recognize that my brain is still in fight or flight mode much of the time and trying to deal with yet more significant change, like moving house, is an enormous ask, especially when life has never seemed so uncertain. I will need to enact full Change Ninja skills if I'm going to pull this off, I tell myself.

I gear myself up for tackling the slightly large elephant in the room which is that I haven't had a conversation with my ex-partner about selling the house or our living situations. The conversation I decide to have is made slightly easier by only talking about the facts (rather than the emotion) in that I can't afford to stay here by myself long term and he can't afford to buy me out. He's very clear he's happy for me to stay in the house for now and is in no rush to sell and while I do want to move ASAP, I decide it's prudent not to mention my plans yet. He doesn't need to know. Yet. It gives me breathing space and it gives me back a little bit of control over the situation. I decide it would be best if I know more than he does, so I can try and manage things in ways that won't cause me any more stress. I call the solicitors to get the process moving again so that the house is ready to sell, something I can do without my ex-partner's permission because we had already started the process. The next step is having photographs taken for the brochure, so I get out the mop bucket to give the house a really good clean, iron the bedsheets, fill the vases with fresh flowers, and declutter all the surfaces as requested by the photographer. The house has never looked so good and a tiny little bit of me wonders if it would be possible to stay here after all. But then I remind myself that staying is the same as procrastinating; it would just be trying to cling on to some of the old life which is gone. I need to be brave, move on, and start again.

A week later and everything is in place to put the house on the market. But something is still holding me back. My fearful brain is kicking in again and again, planting all kind of doubts and 'what if?' worries. I know that doubts are really just thoughts the brain has made up. One of my wing people keeps reminding me they aren't really real. They won't, she reminds me, change actual reality, they are just the brain's way of trying to protect me. 'Sometimes', she says 'the brain gets it wrong. Just think of them as risks and then think of a way to eliminate them. Or sort of ignore them, if you don't look directly at them, they will eventually go away'.

But my brain is in overdrive and imagining not being able to find anywhere to live that would suit me and ending up being homeless if I rush through with the sale of the house. My cautious brain is telling me that it would be much more sensible to have bought somewhere first before I push for the sale. Logically it's a no-brainer and would eliminate some, nay most, of those risks/doubts. If I buy first, I think, then the worst case would be having to pay for two properties concurrently for a few weeks at most as I'm pretty certain that my current house will sell fast. My solicitor has yet again said that this is not a good plan, and I should sell first to be in with a good chance of getting an offer accepted, but what does he know?[26] And it's not him who may end up with nowhere to live.

So, despite my solicitor's sage advice I tell him now is no time for risk taking and that I need to be sensible and logical. I pause the selling (which also pauses the next difficult conversation with the ex-partner about just how quickly I intend to move on with my life) and go off to hunt for somewhere to buy first. At this stage I need some certainty. Life has just thrown me a huge curveball. I'm still experiencing a heightened sense of fear, I'm still full of anxiety and stress hormones and still having to consciously manage my emotions pretty much continuously. I need to know I have somewhere I can live and start my new life and not risk even more uncertainty.

Besides, I think, this should be easy. How hard can it be to buy a wee house in one of the villages I've picked out that would suit me and the dog? OK, so I might only have half the money to spend this time round but I'm not looking for perfect, just a suitable home not too far away but far enough that it feels like the country. I'm still dreaming of farmhouse kitchens, a cottage garden, chickens, and plenty of space, but accept I need to let some of this go, at least for now. I don't *need* anything big or grand. It just needs to meet my needs and feel safe and comfortable.

---

[26] He's only been doing the job for 20 years and only moved house six times!

After a week of looking and finding nothing remotely suitable I become a tad despondent. There is nothing, and I mean nothing available that is suitable or affordable. Rather than panic me though it just deepens my resolve to buy first because the chances of finding something after I've sold will be tiny. I'm not being forced out of the house any time soon and I still haven't told my ex-partner that I intend to get the house sold as soon as possible. I can, I remind myself, take some time on this, I don't need to rush it. But the reality is I end up struggling to motivate myself to do anything other than looking for a house to buy because now that I've decided that's what I'm doing I need, for me, for it to become a reality. I bore everyone I know with my first-world problem, recognizing that in the grand scheme of things I'm still in a very fortunate position. Days seem to crawl by, and I again feel stuck.

It's a Friday morning. I'm not sleeping well and have been awake for three hours forcing myself not to look again at the property sites as nothing will be different from yesterday. I get up and take my dog for a long walk, come back, and make some breakfast while catching up on the news. It's now 9.15 and I can no longer wait so I do a page refresh on the property site and an absolutely perfect house appears. I call up the agents instantly and arrange to visit that afternoon. Work is firmly taking a back seat at this point.

I call one of my wing people and mention that it's top end of my budget but that I really would like to make an offer that would get accepted if it is as good as it looks on paper. They urge me to go high and worry about it later. 'You won't regret it if it's the right place' he advises. I know he's right but it's like I needed someone to give me the permission to maybe spend a bit more than I'd originally planned.

Six hours later and I'm sitting in my car in a layby three minutes from the house. I have 100% fallen in love with it. It's almost perfect, I think. It does have one sizeable fault that is niggling away in my gut but nothing my logical brain is thinking is a deal breaker.[27] It's also, I accept, possibly a little too small for some of my oversized furniture but it's just stuff I tell myself, stuff I can get rid of or replace. I have romanticized the idea of living here so much that I think of a figure to offer and call my solicitor and put in an offer I think

---

[27] This is one of those things where my gut is telling me one thing and my head is choosing a different response. It's not a good idea to ignore the gut but we often do, especially if we feel like a situation is desperate and the brain 'talks' us into a decision and overrides that gut feel.

is unlikely to get knocked back. It's a fair bit over the asking price and they seem to be keen for a quick sale.

It seems rash, especially for me, to make such an expensive life-changing decision so quickly but it feels like it would be a good place to start again. It's in an area I love, has the calm I need but is not too isolated. If I think about it too much I might talk myself out of it and I really do need to take the plunge into the future, to make a decision that I can't reverse. As I drive home, I laugh that it took me nearly a week to pick and commit to a new pair of trainers and I've just made one of the biggest purchase decisions I will ever make in around 20 minutes. But I also know that stasis often comes from having too much choice. When you have a need, and supply is small, you have to move fast.

I start to get excited. There is a chemical cocktail party going on right now in my brain and body. Stressful cortisol and anxiety-inducing adrenaline are ever present, I'm still scared witless, but I'm also motivated to move forward and have that overly exciting anticipation of pleasure feeling that I know comes from dopamine. I remind myself of all of this to help manage the physical feelings, to try and slow down my heart rate. I explain it all out loud to myself to help reduce some of the overwhelming feelings. This helps me accept it which has the knock-on effect of feeling a little less physical stress in my body, enough to at least, be able to drive safely.

I pull into my drive an hour later and the phone rings. It's the solicitor. Such fast news must certainly be good news I think gleefully. Except it isn't. They have rejected my bid and have gone for one that was substantially less money but the buyer had already sold their property so there was no chain, there was cash in the bank and therefore no mortgage to sort out. This house was on the market for less than 24 hours – the vendors went for an easy sale rather than the highest price. This is madness.

My solicitor reminds me again in 'I told you so' tones that I need to sell first, to have the money in the bank or as a minimum have a buyer in the processes of buying my property.

Another crashing defeat. Disappointed and deflated barely cover it and the panic and anxiety ramp up again. I know I need to make a really tough decision and I know that, until I do, then restarting my life is at risk of being on permanent hold. Do I keep going with my logical, risk-reducing plan, to buy before I sell? Or do I follow the solicitor's advice and sell first? A decision that will create absolute and utter uncertainty and have me living in the permanent state of fear that I may have nowhere to live.

I briefly flirt with the third option of renting out the house and maybe heading off to India or somewhere for a year of self-reflection or some other 'finding myself' adventure, but I instantly rule this idea out. I'm not the 'finding myself' type. However much those stories and books about eating and praying and loving sound idyllic or inspiring, a lot of us aren't really cut out for that type of life sabbatical. If we were, we would already be doing it to some degree. Most of us also have other things going on in life we can't just walk away from, work, family and, in my case, a dog. Nor do I have the emotional energy or bandwidth to think about that type of life-changing adventure trip and all that would entail.

So, back to this decision I need to make.

For me, having time to find the right place to start my new life and not risk being homeless means I should buy before I sell. On the other hand, to be able to secure an offer so I can start my new life means I need to have cash in the bank, no chain, and a mortgage lined up.

My dilemma. Sell before I buy or buy before I sell? One route, I'm told, won't lead to success, the other route is one of the most daunting things I can imagine. Even if it's 'only on paper', being homeless is a very scary prospect for me, especially as I don't have much energy and emotional reserves to lean on at this point. I know that for me, I really need a base that I can call mine to be able to deal with all of the other things that are going on. I am stuck, it seems, between a rock and a hard place. And I know just the tool to work this out, HardPlaceRock™.

I make a very large mug of coffee and start by looking at the example I use for teaching this tool. The example is quite a simple one, but it always helps to think through it first before using the tool on something real.

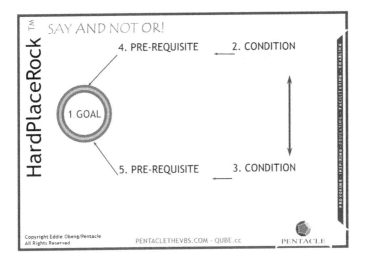

Example: Your goal is to have a happy home.

In order to have a happy home imagine you've made the following assumptions:

Your spouse is always complaining they never see you so you think 'if I spend more time at home, my spouse will be happy and so I will have a happy home'.

On the other hand, your children are complaining that all their friends are going on an exciting holiday somewhere in the sun and you haven't booked anything. You know for a happy home you need to fix this but to be able to afford an exciting holiday you think 'I need more money and that means spending more time at work'.

It seems that, in order to have a happy home, you need to spend more time at home because that will make the spouse happy and more time at work to earn the money to keep the children happy.

It seems it's an impossible situation, doesn't it? It seems that perhaps you are stuck between a rock and a hard place?

I then, even though I know the answers to this scenario already, draw out the example on the tool template because it helps me organize the scenario into the assumptions that have been made.

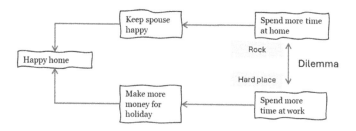

Once I've done this I try and 'break' the assumptions that have been made in the scenario. I start to think about other ways in this scenario that I could make a happy home that makes the spouse and the children happy. The trick is, I know, to break the solid cause and effect arrows.

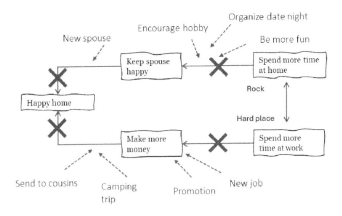

Does the spouse need me at home more or is it about what I do when I'm at home? Perhaps we could try date night, or I could try and be more fun? Perhaps the spouse needs supporting and encouraging in their new hobby? Or should I just get a new spouse? A bit drastic perhaps but it's an option!

Do I need to spend more time at work to earn more money or could I perhaps apply for a different job or a promotion? Do I really need more money for an exciting holiday, or could I borrow some camping equipment and turn the summer into an outdoor adventure holiday or pack the kids off to their cousins for the summer?

By mapping out the original thinking and trying to break each of the assumptions and conditions I'm able to see things differently. It is no longer an impossible dilemma. In this scenario there is no longer a rock or a hard-place decision because I now have other options.

Life ninja move 2

Story: When you are stuck between a rock and a hard place, as my personal dilemma demonstrates, it can be really difficult to know what to do for the best. The fear of making the wrong decision can result in never-ending brain turmoil that tells you it's all impossible. Thinking won't get you out of this situation but looking at your situation from the third person and challenging *all* of your assumptions will.

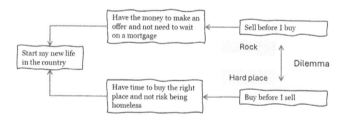

Tool: I want you to practise the Hard-PlaceRock™ tool with my dilemma from the story before applying it to your own dilemma. A bit like I did with the happy home example.

Insights: What did you discover? How have you broken the assumptions? If you were me, what decision are you going to now make based on breaking these assumptions?

If you applied the tool to your own dilemma, what have you discovered? Have you got more information to help you make a decision? How does it feel in your gut?

The trick with this tool is to force your brain to think differently. Thinking differently is really hard to do, but HardPlaceRock™ challenges your thought pathway when you really feel you are in an impossible position.

Reflection: When you have difficult decisions to make it is often because you've made some assumptions that you think *must* be true. You might share these with others, and they might suggest different things, but your mind is often made up and you really can't see a way out, despite their suggestions.

But if you lay this out in a clear way, describing both sides of the dilemma as being impassable and start to ask, 'what else might be true?' you will quickly find that there are some previously unthought of approaches you could take that will still get you to your end goal. You might ask for help with this tool to nudge your thinking a little, but the answer you need really needs to come from you. It needs to feel right.

Points time: For each new 'idea' you came up with for my HardRockPlace™ give yourself a healthy 20 points.

If you applied the tool to your own dilemma gain a further 40 points.

If you applied the tool to your own dilemma and now have a very definite way forward identified and are feeling a huge amount of relief add an additional 40 points. And very well done you!

Health points = _____

I switch on the coffee machine for a refill. I know in my given state coffee is probably the last thing I should be drinking but it both tastes and feels good and I think I deserve a treat. Once the coffee is made, I map out my rock and hard place assumptions.

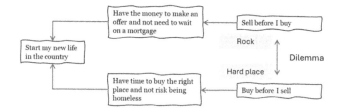

After ten minutes of getting nowhere on what still seems like an impossible dilemma I decide, instead, to take the dog for a walk knowing my brain will work away at this in the background.[28]

About 30 minutes into my walk, I have a eureka moment and quickly head home so I can capture it before I lose it.

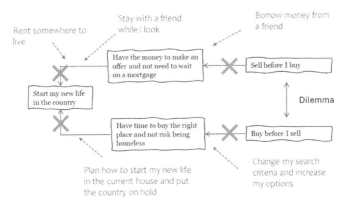

---

[28] This is one of my top tips. Everyone remembers Charles Darwin and his Theory of Evolution but apparently, he got stuck and couldn't work out what it was he'd discovered, even though he knew he had discovered something. He couldn't quite put his finger on what he'd found. So, he put his notes to one side and went on holiday for six months giving it little thought. Then on his return he had his eureka moment that is the theory we all know to this day. When you are stuck on something the worst thing to do is sit staring at the screen trying to work out the answer, the best thing to do is distract your brain (exercise is a great one). Often, you'll find that your brain works out the answer in the background without you giving it much obvious thought at all. If you don't believe me then ask yourselves how many times have you had your best ideas in the shower?

To present myself as 'risk free' to buyers do I really need to have sold or are there other ways to get access to the money on a temporary basis, especially as I have no doubt my house will sell quickly. Do I have any very generous, trusting, and rich friends, for example, who might loan me the money?

While I don't want to make the wrong decision and feel rushed, do I actually really need a lot of time to find somewhere? Am I perhaps still trying to find that dream house in my dream location? Am I ruling things out too quickly because they're not perfect?

Could I sell the house and rent somewhere? Could I stay with a friend? Could I even rent this house and rent somewhere? Could I stay put and come up with an entirely different plan of how to restart my life?

I actually clap my hands with glee. My non-breakable impossible situation is broken.[29] I start to explore these new options.

Of course, I don't have a rich friend who would give me a massive lump sum of money to buy a house, but I do have a friend who offers a bridging loan which would mean I could factor out having to sort a mortgage as part of any house bid, something else that was limiting my chances. And of course, I can't sofa surf with a dog and work to do but a friend does offer temporary accommodation for a few months in

---

[29] On paper this all might seem obvious. Especially as it's not your 'emotional' challenge and your logic for this scenario is most defiantly on. But when you feel in an emotional and impossible situation nothing feels obvious, you just feel very stuck.

an ideal spot which would give me company, is in the country and would perhaps open up other opportunities once I felt a bit less panicky.

I realize that:

a) I am incredibly lucky with my wing people crowd;
b) I have more data to work from to make a decision;
c) my logic is starting to switch back on, and the emotional brain is calming down; and
d) I'm motivated and energized to make a decision. I know exactly what I need to do.

I don't need time to find the 'right' place to live and the 'right' house to live in because I have never ever done this before. I haven't lived in the country or by myself before. So how can I know what the right house is? Does having more time to find the right place help or could it perhaps be a limiting factor? Does having potentially limitless time give me more time to turn things down that would be perfectly adequate? Could it be used to procrastinate over yet another decision?

The decision is made. I'm going to sell the house first because my assumption that I need plenty of time to get the right house in the right area has been broken. I'm eternally optimistic, something will turn up I tell myself and a flood of relief, albeit briefly, washes over me.

Of course, I have copious reservations, including still having an attachment, of sorts, to my current home, nay house, but I have to accept that it's part of the past and no longer part of my future. Staying put is procrastination; it is not moving me forward, nor is it moving me out of the grief and sadness I feel.

Chapter 10

Plans that stick

The decision is made, I'm going to sell the house first. If I change my search criteria and open up my options to more types of houses in more locations, then I surely won't need a lot of time to find somewhere because I'm not looking for perfect. The focus will be more on the goal of starting a new life in the country rather than finding the right house in the perfect location.

Although I'm still full of uncertainty about the future, still dealing with the emotions of what is happening to me (it's only been a few weeks) and I'm utterly exhausted, it feels like progress. However, the thought of what I will now have to do, on top of everything else, in order to actually move house, feels like a mountain to climb. I find myself swearing a lot at my ex-partner (in his absence) but this does, at least, feel a tad cathartic.

I become aware that I need to: (a) try and look after 'me' a bit otherwise I'll become ill; and (b) not become overwhelmed and start panicking about all the things I need to do to move house. Moving house, I know, can be pretty stressful, even in the best of circumstances. Doing it when it feels less like choice, when I don't know where I will end up, when I'm doing it all by myself, when there's still the small risk of finding myself homeless, and when I'm still so very full of grief for what I have lost, could, I know, be a step too far.

I decide that I should write a checklist to help me through the next phase because, if nothing else, I am a little bit clearer on what is going to happen next. It will, I hope, at least help to avoid the major meltdown which is ever threatening.

1. When panic threatens to take over, I practise the physiological sigh (two breaths in, one breath out) which I know will calm me down almost instantly and keep the fight or flight response in check.

2. I run daily. Exercise releases serotonin which increases happiness and reduces anxiety. Exercise releases endorphins which are associated with increased pleasure and reduced stress. Exercise can be mindful or meditative and gives my brain time to process things subconsciously. No matter how low I feel or how much I don't want to run, I go anyway. It is, without doubt *the* best medicine. I never regret a run.

3. I stroke and fuss over my dog a lot more than
    normal to release oxytocin, which makes me feel
    more connected, especially when the loneliness
    kicks in during the evening. I even let her on the
    bed for an early morning cuddle which breaks all
    my usual rules.

4. I notice the time I struggle most, in relation to what
    has happened, is early evening when we would, as
    a couple, have been preparing dinner and talking
    about the day. The anticipation of this habitual
    routine which no longer manifests is painful as it's a
    daily reminder of what I've lost and what I'm grieving
    for. Instead of trying to manage my emotions around
    this I instead try and plan something in every day
    around 5 or 6pm. Ideally outside of the house, like
    meeting friends or doing the shopping. If I'm home,
    then I try and arrange a video call with someone to
    fill that hour. When I change my routine, it removes
    the 'built in' daily anticipation or trigger which in
    turn removes some of the pain.[30] I need to distract
    myself, I think, at this key point in the day.

---

[30] We grieve in time, space, and closeness. Simplistically these three things
are a map of where that person or thing is for us. When something is no
longer there, we grieve, and it hurts. But if we can try and uncouple time
and space then we can start to reduce some of the pain. For example, if we
habitually expect someone to come home at 5pm every day, then our brain
predicts this, and we get a little hit of dopamine from the anticipation of it.
When it doesn't happen, we get pain of the desired thing not happening.
We then remember they're going to be late and relax, or wonder where
they are and panic, or, if they are no longer part of our life, remember that
and the wave of grief hits us again.

5. I reframe the doubts and retell my story. For example:

    If I think, 'The person I thought I could trust unconditionally has forced me into making decisions I never wanted to make, at least by myself', I reframe it as, 'I am now able to pursue my dreams without the need for me to manage someone else's needs, fears and anxieties'.

    Another:

    If I think, 'If only I'd offered even more on that perfect house I might have got it', I reframe it as, 'It would have been a problem house over time because of the limitations for dog walking in the vicinity'.

    I'm not making up things that aren't true (the house was on an estate where dogs needed to be on the lead) but I am seeking a 'what else might be true?' narrative that's more positive. By repeating the reframes they quickly become my reality and so I feel much better. It's very much like magic.

6. I listen to very loud music to stimulate the reward centre in my brain (dopamine).

7. I will manage the house move with my trusty StickySteps™ tool which I know will reduce some of the short-term uncertainty, give me better clarity

on the small chunk of activity I need to focus on *right now* and will give me a regular hit of the feel-good dopamine as I tick things off a to-do list.[31]

8. Oh, and I will try to be nice to myself. Given the circumstances, I am, I think, doing quite well.

I start to write out my StickySteps™ plan beginning with the end goal, my dream vision. The thing at the end of all this horror and pain that will make it all worthwhile. Then I imagine it has already happened, that this imagined future is now my present:

In order to be fully enjoying my new life in the country. I must have…

And then I list the really big chunks of activity I will need to do to make this happen. I write them in the past tense, using a verb at the start which magically turns them into actions.

Next, I order these big chunks to make a sensible high-level plan:

In order to be fully enjoying my new life in the country I must have...

a) Sold the house.
b) Worked out the finances and know what I can afford.
c) Found somewhere to live.
d) Moved house.

---

[31] Just by crossing out things on a list can give you a small boost of 'well done you' feeling.

e) Got to know some of the locals.

f) Bought a tweed jacket and some new posh wellies.[32]

g) Embedded myself into the local community.

And so on.

I now have, in order, a list of big chunks of activity that need to have happened for this new magical life I want. It's a lot. But it's more manageable and less overwhelming than a regular to-do list because the only thing I need to think about and action, *right now*, is the first chunk of activity. Which is to sell the house. The other chunks I can worry about later. Selling the house is still quite a big activity to do and so I repeat the StickySteps™ process by moving the first big chunk to the top line:

In order to have sold the house I must have…

a) Agreed with my ex-partner to put the house on the market.[33]

b) Finalized all the marketing material with the estate agents.

c) Asked the solicitor to add it as a live listing.

---

[32] Ok this is not strictly necessary, but I know in all likelihood this is *exactly* what I will do. I also know that if I don't put this on the plan *and* put it in the right place on the plan, then there's a very good chance I will do nothing *but* look at posh wellies on Google for the next three weeks. And that wouldn't be good.

[33] The elephant again. I really need to have that difficult part of the conversation.

d) Sorted out a dog sitter for the anticipated viewings.

e) Cleared the diary for anticipated viewings.

And so on.

Suddenly it feels incredibly manageable. I have a very nice, neat to-do list I can get on and, well, do. I also know I will get huge, well maybe not huge, but some, satisfaction from ticking these things off as it will trigger the dopamine/reward system in my brain. It's still very scary overall *and* I'm still swearing, a lot, *but* I'm no longer thinking, nay panicking, about all the things I will need to do at some point in the future.

And because I've captured all the big chunks of activity that will need doing in the future, I know I'm less likely to wake up in the middle of the night panicking about all the detailed things I haven't yet put on my list because they will, I know, get listed when I get to the appropriate chunk in the future. For now, I am very clear on what I need to do right now, and they are all things I have some level of control and autonomy over. All of which makes me physically feel much better.

Life ninja move 3

Story: It's a reasonable thing, when planning an activity, to write a to-do list. Like going on holiday for a much-needed break. You need to book flights, book accommodation, book time off work, and you tick them off as you do them. When it comes to the day of your flight you might then start to plan backwards. Let's say you need to be at the airport for a 9am flight. You will, I'm sure, work backward to determine what time you need to leave the house. Boarding at 8.30am, security at 8am, car parked at 7.45am, wiggle room of 30 minutes, and so on, until you realize that you need to get up at 4.30am for a 9am flight. It's only then that you wonder why you thought this would be a good way to start a much-needed break. It's only then you might wonder why you didn't plan the whole thing backward to avoid this ridiculous start.

Tool: Let's look at the holiday to-do list again:

• Ask everyone where they want to go.
• Book time off work.
• Agree a budget.
• Book flights and accommodation.

It looks like a logical list. But if you look again, it's possible you have picked a location, booked time off work only to find you are not only getting up at 4.30am but also losing three days of holiday because there weren't flights to the location you wanted on the days you've booked off. Not so great for the stress-free holiday.

But if you force yourself to work backwards from the overall end goal, using the StickySteps™ template you are much more likely to have that stress-free break.

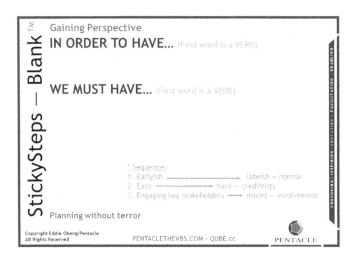

In order to have a relaxing, much needed break I must have:

- Avoided a stressful journey.
- Agreed time off with the boss that works for them and me.

- Agreed a destination with the family that everyone is happy with.

And then, rather than just getting on with all the actions at once you should repeat the exercise for the first step:

In order to avoid a stressful journey, I need to have:

- Researched flight options and times.
- Ensured we don't need to leave the house until 8am.
- Checked out airport transfer options at the other end.
- Ensured we arrive at the destination before 8pm.

Not only will this make for a good travel experience, but it will also provide you with potential dates (to check with work) and potential destinations (to offer the family) which will make the next chunks of activity easier to do and you will have managed the expectations of others. It's a stress-free holiday plan for a stress-free holiday.

 Application: Complete this list of actions:

1. Write down a goal you have just now. It would be great if it is something that feels a little daunting, or something you are procrastinating on.

2. Rewrite the goal to phrase it as if it has already happened. In order to have/be...

3. Check it's future focused and includes the desired outcome. Like the holiday. In order to have had a nice *relaxing* holiday...

4. List the big chunks of activities you will need to have done to achieve this. Focus on just the big chunks for now, not the detail. Remember to use a verb and the past tense to turn it into an action you did to achieve the goal.

5. Put the big chunks in the order you need *to do* them. Not a logical order like biggest things first, but an order that means future actions won't impact on earlier ones and require you to re do them.

6. Check to make sure the chunks are in the right order. Are you sure that first thing comes before all the others? Are you sure that last thing shouldn't be completed sooner? A great example of this is for work projects. People often say they need to write a communication and then work out who the stakeholders are to send it to. Because that sounds logical. But it's the wrong way round. If you don't work out who your stakeholders are *first*, then how do you know what to write and how to communicate? If you're not sure, then try rejigging your big chunks and see if a different order would make better sense.

7. Congratulations! You have an overall plan of the big chunks of things you did to achieve your goal.

8. Now repeat the process by taking the first big chunk on your list and turning that into a goal or outcome, before listing the activities that you will have done to achieve this outcome.

9. Congratulations! You now have a manageable to-do list to get you moving towards your overall goal. If it still feels overwhelming repeat the Sticky-Steps™ process again on the second plan, taking the first chunk of activity from that and creating a third plan.

 Insight: What have you noticed as you have been doing this?

What might have shifted in terms of your to-do list? Perhaps the order you need to do things has changed? Perhaps you now have big activity chunks rather than lots and lots of detail for things far away in the future? Perhaps your detailed list is both small and doable?

Do you feel less anxious about the overall goal? Especially some of the later chunks that are currently quite vague.

Do you have a small action plan that you feel you can start to make progress on for your first chunk of activity?

Reflection: This tool works for all change but is particularly good for the uncertain changes in life that feel much harder, much more overwhelming, and much more panic inducing. These are the things that might keep you awake at night or have you waking up in bed in a panic at 3am. When you plan back from the future, you start to create a level of certainty, autonomy, and motivation to move forward even if the end point still feels a bit vague. Because you are focusing only on the detail of the immediate tasks rather than worrying about the entirety of the change, you start to relax a little. And because you are writing in the past tense then it feels much more achievable because the story you are telling yourself, from the future, is that you have, indeed, achieved your goal. Without StickySteps™ I would have written lists of *all* the things that would need doing for moving house to make sure I didn't forget about them in the future, such as house insurance and new vets. And that list would have quickly become both unwieldly *and* overwhelming.

By having big chunks of activity set out in a timeline, one of which is called 'moved house', then I know that when it gets closer to actually moving house, I will do a StickySteps™ for all the activities I need to do to have successfully moved house, including things like insurance, and finding a vet.

As you complete the detail of your first chunk of activity you should also remember to physically tick things off the list and celebrate that fact that you have done them. This will give you a small dopamine and endorphin hit, a brain-friendly reward, which will give you energy and motivation to do the next thing.

 **Points time:** 30 points for each sticky step plan you manage to produce for your own challenges and an extra 10 points if you start the plan immediately and feel like 'yes, you've got this'.

Health points = _____

Chapter 11

Decisions, decisions

My StickySteps™ plan and ongoing support from wing people has helped suppress the panic a little, enough at least to be able to start to tackle my 'manageable' to-do list. And after a very difficult chat with my ex-partner, we agree to put the house on the market.

It's Thursday, the day after the house went on the market and there are 15 viewings booked in for the weekend. My gut instinct that the house would sell quickly seems to be playing out. I set to getting the house ready, cleaning, ironing bed linen, filling vases with flowers, and turning my old home into someone else's dream property.

At 11am on Friday I take the dog for a very long walk before popping her and her bed in the boot of the car.[34] She will sleep for a few hours while I have four back-to-back viewings.

I prepare my story because viewers are certain to ask why I'm moving, and I know that the way I tell the story could affect their impression of the house. I'm pretty sure a tale of 'we're splitting up' will give the impression I'm desperate for a sale and could lead to lower offers. My story, I decide, will be one of adventure, a move to the country, perhaps chickens and a small holding. 'We love this house', I will say, 'but we are ready for a change'. It's not difficult for me to say 'we' in the story. In fact, it's incredibly hard to say 'me', I've been a 'we' for such a long time. And it really still is my ultimate dream even though I can't imagine it as my next step, not in its entirety at least.

By the third viewing I realize that I'm starting to feel a bit excited. Telling the story the way I am is starting to make it feel more real (in the good way). I'm moving to the country I think, for a new life and adventure. For the first time since this whole thing happened, I can see a glimmer of hope and happiness somewhere in the future. This is aided by the third couple asking if they can come back on Sunday for a second viewing.

By Monday afternoon, after constant viewings on Saturday and Sunday I accept a pretty generous offer. Even the solicitor is surprised at the speed of the sale and the amount offered. I quickly agree a move-out date

---

[34] Panic ye not. She has a bed, water, toys, and fresh air. She thinks she's going on a trip so is more than happy.

without too much thought and heave a sigh of relief. I then dig out my calendar before swearing loudly. I've just agreed to a six-week turnaround. Six weeks! To find and buy somewhere new to live. I breathe and try to hold back the panic that's threatening to set in again. It's definitely time, I think, to avoid any dementors, the ones who are likely to tell me it will all be fine and not to panic because while this might be true, hearing that from them won't, at this point, be in any way helpful.

And so, I start again with my frantic search for a place that might work for me. I have definitely ruled out staying in the city for all the reasons I wanted to move out of the city in the first place. I also know I can't really afford to live in the city now I only have half the money! I'm still craving the quietness of country life but don't want to feel isolated, which is a real threat, especially when I think about winter, stormy weather, and all the things that can happen in the middle of nowhere. I need some outdoor space but also want it to be manageable, and it needs to be near a train station for work. Ideally, I want something I can just move into without needing any renovation work as at this point, I don't have any energy for more disruption. I've done some research and picked out a couple more areas that could work for me.

As I look again and again for what I don't think is a tall ask, the market suggests otherwise and seems to be mocking me. There is nothing that would remotely suit my lifestyle and the needs that I have.

A week later and I start to panic a little. Stay calm, I think and practise the 'physiological sigh' breathing technique, a lot!

By Wednesday the breathing is no longer working. Well, it might if I could do it but I'm in full blown fight or flight mode. I'm not functioning well, have lost my appetite, can't focus, and seem to be permanently thirsty. All indicators suggesting that 'Houston, we have a problem'.

I know I'm lucky and this is far from being homeless in any sense, but for me, in this moment, it feels like I'm homeless. Home, for me, is where I'm grounded, from where I can, if I feel safe, do just about anything. So, the thought of having no home is terrifying. I look at the rental market to see if that's an option, but it doesn't seem that it will be much easier, especially with a dog. I do venture out to see a couple of rental properties that I know aren't really suitable at all, but I am feeling desperate. I arrive at them only to find about 20 other couples visiting at the same time. Demand is high and supply is low.

On Thursday I'm in such a panicky state I consider taking the house off the market. When I let my ex-partner know this, he's a bit too happy and encourages me to do so.

I realize this is time for the emergency help button. This is time for the wing person I've kept in reserve until now. I call Eddie.[35]

---

[35] Colleague, mentor, friend, guru. The Eddie who invented many of the tools in this book and who features heavily in (shameless plug) *The Change Ninja Handbook*.

I explain I'm in a real state of panic and don't know what to do for the best.

'OK', he asks, getting straight to business, 'What's the *issue*? What's causing the stress?'

'I've sold the house and need to be out in just a few weeks and have nowhere at all lined up to move to. I've got the dog to think about, a house full of furniture that likely won't fit into a small place, I can't think straight, can't  work, and I am just panicking. I need somewhere to feel safe so I can start getting on with life again. I think my only option is to take the house off the market and pause the move.'

'You've got loads of time' he reassures me. 'You can do anything in four weeks. But first, who do you need to consider? The main *stakeholders* if you like. Who are they?'

'Me, the dog, clients who I have deadlines for, my bank manager. I think that's it.' I reply.

'What about me, and the team? We need you functioning and working too.'

'Ah yes' I laugh, 'I guess you are also *stakeholders*'.[36]

'OK, next, what's the *outcome* you want?' he continues.

---

[36] When we do this type of thing for personal life changes it can be really easy to miss out people who are close to us when we think about stakeholders. But those close to us might be impacted, good or bad, by any decisions we make. Make sure you capture them all.

'To find somewhere that could feel like home, that would feel safe, allow me to settle into working out what life would look like and that has all my basic needs.'

'Great', he responds. 'Now go and think about all the options you could have and then think about what will happen *next* if you choose that option. And make sure you really think through what will actually happen, not just what the end outcome might be. Let me know when you've got your answer.'

And with that he hangs up.

I feel marginally better. He hasn't told me what my answer is based on what he would do but he has guided me to get the right answer for myself using his decision-making tool called ISWON™ that works you through **I**ssue, **S**takeholders, **W**hat outcome you want, **O**ptions, and what will happen **N**ext.

I quickly think of all the possible options:

Option 1: Remove the house from the market and stay in the city house (for now).

Option 2: Rent a property in the country to test out country living before committing all of my money.

Option 3: Expand the search even wider and be much more flexible about both the area and the types of property I look at.[37]

Option 4: Get a camper van and head to Europe for the summer with the dog and work from the van.

---

[37] Even though I don't think I *am* being that picky I *do* accept the number of unknowns about my future, combined with me almost getting my dream house, has possibly reduced the pool of potential I'm looking at.

Life ninja move 4

Story: If you've ever done an options appraisal at work this might, at first glance, seem pretty run of the mill. First describing each option before thinking about the risk, benefit, and cost of each of the options. But typically, and now's the time to be honest, if you have ever done an options appraisal, I'm guessing you secretly already had a preference and sandwiched it in between a low-cost/low-benefit option and an all-singing-all-dancing, but high-cost option to ensure your preferred option is the one that is picked. I'm right, aren't I?

You may also take a similar approach for life challenges too. Most of us won't select a high-risk option because, well, it's too risky. Instead, we watch others take risks on TV shows from the comfort of our sofa. We might say, 'I'd love to do something like that' but mostly do absolutely nothing about it because in the second half of the show it often goes horribly wrong. We then say things like 'idiots' before putting the kettle on for a nice cup of tea.

Remember that first summer holiday after lockdown and needing a holiday with the kids?

Your options were a staycation, holiday in the UK, or to head off for an all-inclusive in the sun. A staycation after lockdown probably sounded like the worst option and an all-inclusive holiday in the sun like the perfect option.

But what if, instead of thinking about the best and worst option you instead thought about would happen next and what you would need to do using the ISWON™ tool? Let's work through what this might look like.

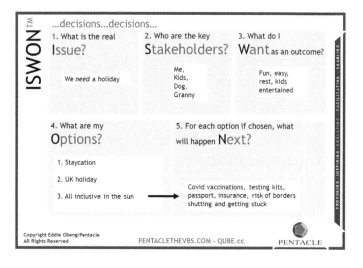

Holiday in the sun: Covid passports, vaccinations, tests, risk of getting stuck somewhere if borders shut down.

UK holiday: Lots of places still shut, regular testing still needed, risk of poor weather, and kids bored without their Xbox.

A staycation: Organize some day trips, get in lots of picnic food, manage days out by what's open and the weather, kids will entertain themselves at home if there's nowhere to go.

Then you might just find a staycation suddenly seems like the perfect option.

Options appraisals in real life, of doing the medium risk, medium benefit, medium cost option, really isn't the best way to make decisions. The best way is to work out what will *actually* happen next for each option. Only then will you know what you are letting yourself in for and know what to expect. Only then will you know, in your gut, what the right decision is for you. And only when it feels right are you likely to choose what on paper looks like a riskier option but, when you are armed with all the information, might just be the best option. For you.

Tool: Imagine you are me in this scenario and using your current decision-making process pick which of the four options below would be the best option. Circle it.

Option 1: Remove the house from the market and stay in the city house (for now).

Option 2: Rent a property in the country to test out country living before committing all my money.

Option 3: Expand the search wider and be much more flexible about both the area and the types of property I look at.

Option 4: Get a camper van and head to Europe for the summer with the dog and work from the van.

Application: Now for each of the four options in my story write down what will happen next, considering each of the stakeholders (me, my dog, Eddie and the team, my bank manager). Don't think about the end outcome but instead capture what will happen, actions and feelings, for each option, and what I would need to do as a result.

If you'd rather, you can, of course, work on your own decision immediately but practicing this tool on someone else's problem is a good way to, well, practice. If you work on your own decision then list out the **Issue**, your **Stakeholders**, what you **Want** next, your **Options** and then what will happen **Next** for each option (considering the impact on stakeholders).

Insight: What new information do you now have that you might have missed for either my options or your own decision?

For each ISWON™ you have done, what option might you now choose based on the information you now have? Does it differ from your initial thinking based on risk and outcome? Has it helped you to make a decision?

Reflection: When making decisions you are more likely to look at the end point rather than *how* you got to an end point. You may have imagined how all possible end points will be – often with rose-tinted spectacles – for the ones you romanticize about or by picturing your terrible future from the seemingly risky options. Of course, you want to avoid risk where possible, but you may need to take some risk to get to the right end point for you. But until you work out what will happen next, in addition to capturing the pros and cons, you might just mislead yourself, to keep you theoretically safe and end up making the wrong decision.

Points time: How well do you think you've captured what will happen next?

Collect 10 points for each of my options you created a 'what next?' for.

Get 10 points if this information changed your mind about the best option.

Get a further 20 points if you completed the tool for your own personal decision and a further 20 points if you have made a real-life difficult decision, one that you now feel very confident about making.

Health points = _____

Time again, I think, for a rewarding coffee before I complete the 'what next?'. I then spend a good 30 minutes working on this as it's so very important to get it right as this decision will determine the next phase of my life. This is what I discover:

Option 1: Remove the house from the market and stay in the city house (for now).

What will happen next? I will need to pay the solicitors for the work to date; it will be harder to start a new life; it will be harder to cut ties with the recent ex; until I do cut ties it's going to be hard to move forward and I might be tempted to move backwards; I will have to let down the people who are buying my house and who I know have already sold their house; I'll be demotivated which will make work all the more harder.

Option 2: Rent a property in the country to test out country living before committing all my money.

What will happen next? I will need to find somewhere that will accept dogs and isn't a minimum term let; I will find it harder to make an effort to settle into a new community if it feels temporary; I might feel isolated if I don't connect with people; I might need to put my furniture in storage; I will feel resentful that I'm wasting money on rent; it will require a lot of effort which could get in the way of my actual paid work and I may feel like I'm letting the team down.

Option 3: Expand the search wider and be much more flexible about both the area and the types of property I look at.

What will happen next? New unthought of possibilities might suddenly become available; it might start to feel more like an exciting adventure if I throw caution to the wind a little; I might start to feel a little less resentful that I'm not getting my dream house in a dream location if I buy something quite removed from that initial dream; an adventure will motivate and energize me so I can still carry out my work commitments.

Option 4: Get a camper van and head to Europe for the summer with the dog and work from the van.

What will happen next? There will be lots of things to arrange (storage of furniture, finding a van, sort out mobile Wi-Fi, getting a dog passport); it might be quite hard to work from a van which might lead to less work coming in; I might feel quite isolated away from my support network; I will likely still feel quite unsettled and end up crying a lot.

A wave of relief floods over me. I pretty much hadn't thought through any of this in the practical way before I used the tool. Because of the panic, I was in full emotional mode and really had assumed the only decision I could or should make was to stay put, at least for now because this seemed like the safest and least risky option. This exercise brings me back from the brink, and dare I say creates a glimmer of hope and excitement again. I know exactly what to do and it's not at all what I expected.

The phone rings. It's Eddie. 'So, what did you discover?' I share my insights.

'Option 1 was to take the house off the market and stay put for a bit longer. This was what I thought I would decide because it's the easiest to do, and, on paper, the lowest risk. But it is definitely the worst decision I could make for me just now. It would, at best, postpone what I need to do and could possibly make things much worse as I could end up taking a step backwards.

Option 2 was to rent and while again, on paper, seems like a low risk and logical option I'm pretty sure I will struggle to commit to settling in the area I end up in because it will feel temporary. And I know I'll resent spending money on rent.

Option 3 was to cast the net wider, be open to any possibility and just pick somewhere that meets my basic needs. This makes it feel more like an adventure I'm *choosing* to do and will hopefully give many more options.

Option 4 was to head off for the summer in a camper van which, while exciting, feels like too much of an adventure for now and will also require a lot of effort to put in motion, furniture storage, buying a van, getting a dog passport. I'm exhausted just thinking about it.

And so, it can only be option 3. I need to cast the net much wider in terms of location and type of property.'

'Perfect' Eddie replies, 'I knew you'd make the right decision. Speak later' and the line, again, goes silent.

I reflect on what has just happened. I've gone from panic and indecision to being very clear on what I'm going to do next, and I waste no time in clearing my filters off the property search engine, hitting the refresh only to find a lot of properties I'd either missed or dismissed quickly pop up. This time I scrutinize the properties from a new perspective. Instead of looking at what's missing from my 'must have' list, I instead ask myself, 'what could life be like living here?'

A few hours later and I spot something, which while definitely a bit pricier than I'd like has me howling with glee. Could I really live somewhere like this, I think? It is as far removed from a country cottage as possible, in an area I'd pretty much dismissed previously but, if this were one of those TV property shows, it would be described as a mystery house. I waste no time in calling the agents and agree to go and see it the following day.

'Wow!' I think as I pull into the drive the next morning. Just wow! It really is as far removed from my previous ideas of country living as possible and yet it could be absolutely perfect for just now. Not perfect for the old me, old life, and old dreams, but perfect for working out what the new me, new life, and new dreams for me are. It may not be a forever home but it's an absolutely perfect transition home. It's both pricey and bonkers but I can't stop smiling. It *feels* like an adventure house. I put in a cheeky bid before I even leave the grounds of the property, but it really is all I can afford. I don't expect the offer to be accepted and know it's highly unlikely this will become my new home, but I also know that I will find something. I've shifted my mindset enough and something will turn up and turn up soon. I decide not to head straight home but go and have a look around the local village and nearest town because I've never even visited this area before. I've just offered all my money (and some!) for a crazy house in a location I've never visited. It all feels a little mad but in a pretty good way.

I head into a coffee shop and order a cappuccino and a Portuguese custard tart which was not what I was expecting in a sleepy town and as I sit down at the table my phone rings. My offer on the mystery house has, it seems, been accepted. I almost cry with relief. I have somewhere to call home.

Chapter 12

Magic box of tricks

It's a couple of days later and things are progressing fast. I jump between feelings of 'eeek', 'phew', and 'yay'. The doubts keep rattling around and the dementors are in full attack mode (i.e., dismissing my crazy decisions and telling me I'm making a mistake) but I swiftly bat off any naysayers (people or thoughts in my head) and focus on doing all the things on my list to keep me in as brain-friendly a space as possible.

Then on day three, well night three, at the devil's hour of 3am I find myself sitting bolt upright in bed, sweat is lashing off me thinking 'what have I done?' A crazy house in a crazy location that only a crazy person would buy. What if I hate it and can't sell it? What if I can't afford the repayments? The thoughts go round and round and round and no amount of breathing calms me down. I have a genuine pit of the stomach fear of getting stuck in an awful situation and the more the night progresses the worse I feel. At 6am I decide it's not too early to message Emily, my coach buddy, and ask if she's free before work for ten minutes. I suspect I know how to get rid of this, what feels like a huge doubt, but the knowledge is buried deep and I need help to pull it out. I need to be coached. At 6.30am she responds and suggests a call at 8am.

I get up and take the dog out, pop the kettle on, and wait for the phone to ring.

Hi, I say, ignoring any niceties, and jumping straight to explaining, nay babbling, my latest panic about ending up stuck with a house I hate, in an area I hate, with all my money (and some) invested in it, and not being able to sell it. Emily asks a few questions to clarify what I've said and then starts coaching me with 'How might you...?' or 'What else could you do if that happens?' type questions. Nothing complex, and on paper it seems very simple, but it's quite hard to do on yourself, especially if you're in a state of emotional turmoil.

'Oh wait!' I suddenly shout out 15 minutes later. 'In the absolutely worst, worst, worst case scenario that I don't like living there and find I can't sell it I will simply rent it out and go live somewhere smaller and cheaper using the rent money. Or head off in a camper van with the dog picking up some house sitting as I go.' This last option was, I remember, an option I had dismissed earlier but could, I know, be a pretty good adventure to do once I felt a bit more settled into a new life.

'In fact,' I continue 'this solution could also potentially make enough money to cover my bills during the winter if I rent it as a holiday let, so it might actually not just be a get out of jail card but could be a reasonably sound business idea too'.

'I can't believe it took you so long to get there' Emily laughs in her Australian drawl.

I join in with the laughter. Another huge weight is lifted. And I compliment her on her very excellent coaching skills. Not once did she hint at this solution and if she had I may have dismissed or created excuses not to explore it. This was one solution I really needed to discover myself to make sure it wasn't just a logical solution but also a solution that had a good gut feeling to it. I managed, with some excellent coaching, to turn meltdown panic into a potential money-making opportunity.

We bid our farewells and I reflect on how much lighter I feel, lighter than I've felt in weeks. I'm buying a crazy house in a place I have very little knowledge of, and it will be *just fine*.

Life ninja move 5

Story: When you are in a panic about something it's hard to focus on what you should do because panicking seems much easier. This is when you need your coach wing person. They need to draw out your own insights so you can come to your own conclusions about what the answer is. The last thing you need is someone telling you the answer to your problem.

For example, imagine you want to do more exercise to get fit but are struggling to make anything stick. You complain about it to a friend, and they suggest you get up early and go for a run before work because that works for them. You tried that and it didn't work. Another friend suggests you go to the gym after work and before dinner, because guess what? That works for them. You try that too and it doesn't work. Failing to do things other people say are easy is not going to help you achieve your goal but is likely to make you feel like a failure. Especially when those friends start to get fed up with you *not* fixing your problem with *their* easy solution. Instead, you need to work out, for yourself, *when* is a good time for you to exercise and *what type* of exercise might be the right type for you. For that you need new insights about you or the situation.

When you are in a panic the last thing you need is someone else telling you the answer to your problems. Even if the answer sounds logical, it's someone else's answer to your problem and they are not you. For the panic-inducing emotional problems you have, the best solution is to find your own answer yourself, because it is in there, you just can't see it for the panic.

 **Tool:** Now is the time to reach out, possibly beyond your normal reach for exactly the right person who can coach you. Sometimes someone who doesn't know you that well will make the best coach. Ask around if anyone knows any good coaches if you are struggling. See if you can barter some time for something they need.

But if you are struggling to find someone who can fulfil this role then the MagicBoxOfTricks™ tool can help you to get the answers yourself by asking yourself what someone else would do in your situation. It helps you shift your mindset and you start to see lots of other solutions your panicked brain is not able to find.

First you describe what you are trying to achieve. If we use my example that would be:

Having a way to live somewhere else if I hate the house and area and can't sell it.

Next you pick five random characters, famous people, or types of people. For my example let's choose:

- Steven Spielberg
- An entrepreneur
- Florence Nightingale
- Madonna
- Agatha Christie

Then ask yourself, 'what would each of these characters do in my situation?' before converting their answer into something practical you could actually do.

Steven Spielberg might use it for his next film. Could I offer it up as a location for TV and films? It is an historic property after all.

An entrepreneur might use it for their business. Could I use it to run workshops and residentials for my business?

Florence Nightingale might rent the house out and go and work in a war zone. Could I rent it and go travelling in that campervan after all?

Madonna might use the place as her summer yoga retreat. Could I let the space to others wanting to run retreats in the country?

Agatha Christie might use it as the plot for her next murder mystery. Perhaps this might be the time to really get stuck into those half-written novels.

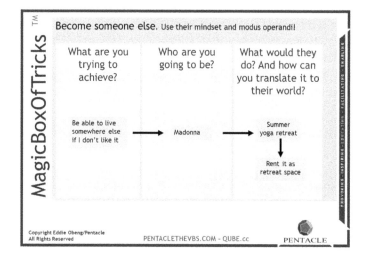

Application: Now it's your turn.

1. Think about a dilemma or problem you are stuck on and what it is you'd like to achieve.
2. List five different characters, famous people, or types of people.
3. Put yourself in their shoes and ask what they would do in your situation.
4. Turning their idea into something you could do in your world.

 Insight: Did you get fresh ideas, different thinking, nudge you toward something that feels right in your gut?

Reflection: You can't think yourself out of a problem with the same thinking that got you there.

A coach, especially one that doesn't know you well, will help you think differently and pull out fresh ideas and insights from within you that will lead you to your own 'eureka' moment. One that will feel right. But if you can't get access to a coach then use MagicBoxOfTricks™ to help you think about your problem from a different perspective. If you get stuck you can do this with someone else because they won't be directly giving you what they think is the solution, they will be thinking of the solution from the characters' perspectives. You can then use these ideas as prompts for something you might do. This tool is a great way to get some fresh insights and practical solutions quickly.

Points time: 20 points per 'What would X do?'

20 points per idea you've converted into a potential action you could do.

20 bonus points if you have a clear decision and feel calmer.

Health points = _____

Chapter 13

The fog begins to lift

Finally, after three months of lots of challenging, life changing, emotional, and often terrifying decision making about things that will affect the rest of my life, the fog really is starting to lift. It's moving day. I've reached the point in my journey where there has been so much stress and change that I almost no longer notice it. This is the start of a new me and a new life, even if I still have no real idea what the future holds. The removal men came two days ago, and I spent all of yesterday cleaning the house.

I'm now loading the last few bits into the car, including the dog, and have one last look around. I expected I'd feel sad at this point but without anything in it I see the house for what it is. A bunch of square rooms. It's no longer 'home'. This, I think, is all boding well. Of course, the adrenalin is pumping again, I'm about to embark on a huge change, but it's a mix of nerves and nervous excitement.

I lock the door, wave a final goodbye to the neighbour, take a deep breath, strap in, and switch the car ignition on. Wow. A new life, I think. Woahhhh! I am really finally doing this. I have a couple of hours' driving ahead and have plenty of time as I'm last in the chain for collecting keys. I've been told it will be about 2pm before I hear from anyone. My plan is to find somewhere for lunch and go for a nice walk as it's an absolutely perfect spring day.

As I pull onto the motorway the phone rings. It's the buyers of my house. This can't be good, I think. I hit the accept button on the car computer and try not to panic.

'Have you heard?' he asks with a real sense of urgency.

'What?' I reluctantly ask, thinking the worst, that the chain has fallen through. 'Stay calm' I tell myself as I almost veer onto the hard shoulder.

'There's a problem with the money', he continues, 'our buyers' bank has been slow paying us and so it's slowed everything down by a couple of hours'. He sounds really irate and carries on ranting. I start laughing with relief. After all I've been through in the last 12 weeks or so this is so tame it's not even registering. I will have time for lunch *and* coffee, I think, and it will be an opportunity to explore the nearest town which, until now, I've only visited once.

I say thanks for letting me know and that I hope the move goes well for them before hanging up. The relief I felt when knowing there wasn't a real issue is, I know, my gut telling me I'm doing the right thing.

It's 4pm and I finally get the keys and open the door of my new home with excitement. The removal van is due in the morning and so my plan is to clean the house top to bottom. As I wander around, soaking in the space I'm grateful to see that it is already pretty clean, and I realize I'm pretty knackered. And so, I decide to just give the kitchen cupboards and bathroom a wipe down so I can unload things as they are brought in. Once that's done, I blow up the air mattress that will be my bed tonight, dig out the nicely chilled bottle of wine I picked up earlier and head out onto the small terrace at the back of the house. The sky is a glorious shade of blue, the evening sun is still full of spring warmth, the birds are tweeting in the trees, there is not, I realize, the faintest sound of traffic. And I finally feel safe.

I'm about to head back into the house to make a light supper when my immediate neighbour comes out to say hello before helpfully giving me his Wi-Fi code to use until I get connected and to let me know to knock if I need anything else. It bodes well.

It's Tuesday, 19th April, the first day of this new life[38] and my very good friend Susan arrives to help unpack, bringing with her a substantial picnic lunch for us both. I assign her to the lounge while I do the kitchen and we unpack as the boxes are brought in. We hang the pictures randomly on the hooks that have been left, books are put straight onto the bookshelf, clothes go straight into the built-in wardrobe, my home office is set up in 15 minutes, furniture is rebuilt, and outdoor stuff all goes to the garage. By 4pm 80% of the boxes are empty and back on the removal van and I wave the hard workers off. Being surrounded by my things makes it feel much more like my home. OK, so the pictures aren't in the right place yet, but they are up, and it feels cosy and familiar.

I drop Susan at the station (I did get my 'station in half an hour's drive' need met) and pick up something for dinner on the way back from the delightful bakery and deli shop I've discovered in the village.

I head back out to the terrace; this time I have a chair to sit on and think perhaps a glass of celebratory wine would not go a miss. The neighbour waves over and I ask them if they'd like to join me. I fetch a

---

[38] I mention this specific date because it comes to hold some significance later.

spare glass (all unpacked!) and we spend an hour chatting; I find out about all the other neighbours in this small community. We even discover we know some of the same people from our work environments. Small world!

It's 6am the next morning and I wake up with sun streaming through the window, a window which has the same glorious view as the terrace and as I lie just taking it all in, I start to think about what I should do next. The last few weeks have been so busy focusing on house-moving plans (which inevitably wasn't as smooth going as it could have been[39]) but it's all done, and I feel a sense of relief and peace. For about ten seconds. And then the next wave of anxiety hits. I've just moved to an area where I know nobody nor even know the area, I've never lived alone before, never lived in the country before, and have a huge dislike of group activities, especially as a way to meet people. And while the house is 'unpacked' and has a nice feel to it I really do want to make it more 'me' in terms of décor.

---

[39] Like having moving dates agreed, removals booked, everything loaded onto a van *before* the actual contracts were signed because it was a bank holiday weekend. Four days of being in limbo in an empty house not knowing if the sale would go ahead did not make for a relaxing Easter.

Suddenly I feel that there's a lot to do and that I will need a lot of energy and positivity. So much so that I'm tempted, again, to hide under the duvet and pretend everything is just fine because this might, just might, be the biggest mistake I've ever made. Everything about my life still feels so uncertain, and while moving house provided a distraction from these feelings they are now back in full swing. Should I, I wonder, just try and find that energy and focus on making the house really feel like mine? I know the brain likes the familiar, and some of this uncertainty is driven from everything being unfamiliar. Would making this house look more like my expectations of my home reduce the level of uncertainty I'm feeling. Would it provide a feeling of safety, security, and normality for me?

No, I think. It's time to focus on the things that aren't bothering me. By trying to make things more certain, all I will think about is how uncertain things are. I need to distract myself from even thinking about the uncertainty. And one thing I know I'm not currently worried about, at all, is making new pals!

Life ninja move 6

Story: Can you think back to a time you felt utterly deflated, due to maybe something negative your boss said about your work? Or perhaps you found out about a night out that you weren't invited to, and you had that FOMO[40] feeling? Or maybe a merger was announced at work and the uncertainty of what would happen created a real sense of panic. This feeling is caused by social pain and your brain interprets social pain in the same way as physical pain. Whether this is a big announcement at work, feeling embarrassed from having loo paper on your shoe, being patronized, or being left out of a group activity. The brain will perceive the event just in the same way as physical pain and it triggers a response that can leave you feeling just as bad as if you'd broken your leg.

Tool: The SCARF model[41] is a useful tool to use when social pain is a potential problem because it can help you manage this pain. SCARF is an acronym for the most common domains of social pain:

- Status
- Certainty

---

[40] Fear of missing out.
[41] Dr David Rock, NeuroLeadership Institute (NLI).

- Autonomy
- Relatedness
- Fairness

When (social) change happens your brain predicts what will happen next based on your previous experiences. It's more likely than not that it will perceive the change as a potential threat triggered by one or more of these domains. Typically, you have one or two that are triggered more than the others and one that is triggered less often. But any situation can trigger any or all of the domains.

Status – when your personal status is challenged such as being put down, or having your work criticized.

Certainty – when you don't know what the outcome of a change will be, such as redundancies being announced.

Autonomy – if you feel you are losing your autonomy, such as being micromanaged or having decisions made for you.

Relatedness – when you feel left out, such as when friends meet up and don't invite you.

Fairness – when someone is treated more favourably such as a team member getting a pay increase with no explanation.

Imagine job cuts have been announced. You might be triggered by certainty (will it be you?) and possibly fairness (the bosses all just got a significant pay rise). Your first thought might be to try and find more information out to reduce the uncertainty even though it's highly probable there is no information to find out (yet). But by focusing on the thing that is triggered you are at risk of increasing the pain, rather than reducing it,[42] especially if there's a good chance you won't be able to influence or remove the stressor (job losses) that is causing the pain.

If, instead, you focus on actions in relation to the least triggered domain, let's imagine for this scenario that is relatedness and autonomy, you will find the pain often reduces. For example, you may get together with colleagues (relatedness) for a moan but also a laugh, agreeing that you're going to put your feet up for the day (autonomy) as you realize you are all in the same boat. When the pain starts to reduce, you will find you start to think more logically and rationally about the change, you might start to think of other things you could do. You might, for example, use this as an opportunity to update your CV (autonomy) and explore other job options (status). Quickly you will find that rather than panicking about the (uncertain) future or ranting about how unfair it is you will, instead, find that the feelings of fear and anxiety start to reduce because your brain isn't focused on trying to fix the thing you can't fix. Not only will you start to feel better, but you'll be in a much better place to think of this change as an opportunity (a nudge to get a better job) rather than a threat.

---

[42] It's no different to the annoying person at the cinema with sweet wrappers that once you hear becomes incredibly loud and ruins the film for you.

Applying this model gives your subconscious brain breathing space because it's focused on more positive and rewarding activities you can control rather than the stressor you have little influence over.

 Application: Think about the last time something happened or someone said something to you, and you felt that immediate inner 'grrrrrrr', the flush of anger or panicky knot in your tummy. Perhaps you started to get angry or became defensive?

Looking at the SCARF domains can you order them in terms of what was triggered in this scenario you are remembering? With 1 being the most triggered and 5 being the least.

Rank (1–5)	What you did
Status	_____
Certainty	_____
Autonomy	_____
Relatedness	_____
Fairness	_____

Now write down what you did to try and feel better, to try to remove the stress that caused the response.

I'm guessing you tried to feel better by challenging the stress directly. So, if your autonomy was challenged you perhaps tried an action that was a bit 'you can't tell me what to do', if it was status, you perhaps asserted some authority and if it was uncertainty you tried to find out more information. This is normal behaviour but it's unlikely to alleviate the pain and might even make it worse.

What you can do instead is think of, and do, an action in relation to the least triggered domain. This will not only distract you from the stressor that you might have very little control over but will move you away from the pain and might even get rid of the thing that's causing you pain in a different way. It allows you to focus on changing your environment rather than focusing on what's causing the stress.

Let's have another go at this:

- Think of something very current that's causing some stress, anything from job uncertainty to an overflowing inbox.
- Rank the SCARF domains for this particular thing.
- Come up with an action against the least triggered domain.
- Do the action and reflect on how you feel in a few days.

Insight: Have you recognized a domain that is triggered more than the others, and realized how you behave when this is triggered?

Perhaps it's how you respond to people trying to micromanage you? Or perhaps you see 'helpful feedback' more as a criticism and an attack on your status. Do you have an action you think you could do, based on non-triggered domains, that might shift your response the next time it happens? Does it feel like you will feel less stressed if you do this?

And what about that change that might be going on right now? What's not triggered? What will you do to distract yourself from the pain, move you away from the 'fear', and also change the environment around you to remove the impact of the stressor?

 Reflection: Recognizing which of your SCARF domains are most often triggered can have an immediate effect for dealing with the day-to-day things that happen and that cause that 'grrrrr of anger' or 'eeeek' of fear feeling in the pit of your stomach.

If you respond to similar things in the same way every time, then it's likely you are directly responding to the social pain trigger.

Step 1: Recognize it.

Step 2: Label it. 'I feel angry because I'm being micromanaged'. You will find that even simply noticing it and saying it will reduce the pain.

Step 3: Identify what's not triggered.

Step 4: Identify an action that's related to the non-triggered domain.

For example, if you are being micromanaged and autonomy is triggered but relatedness is not then you might call up your colleague and say, 'the boss is at it again, trying to plan my schedule', you both groan and laugh come up with a nickname for them. Over time you will notice much less pain when being micromanaged because you will remember the nickname and laughter. The stressor hasn't changed. You just changed how you responded which reduces the impact it has on you.

 **Points time:** 20 points for completing your typical SCARF profile and finding an action you can do that's associated with your non-triggered domain to shift your typical response and behaviour.

20 points for completing a SCARF profile on your current challenge and finding an action you can do that's associated with the non-triggered domain.

20 points if you come back in a week and realize the thing you are stressing about, while still there, is no longer feeling quite so angst ridden.

An extra 20 points if you end up laughing like a loon in a weeks' time wondering what on earth you were worried about in the first place.

Health points = _____

As I lie in bed thinking again about how uncertain my future seems, going from a shared home in the city with a predictable future to living alone in the country where anything could happen, I reflect that this would be great time to put the SCARF model into practice. I order the domains in terms of how triggered they are:

1. Uncertainty – my whole life has changed.
2. Autonomy – I feel I was forced into this new life, at least the single bit.
3. Fairness – I didn't do anything wrong and yet I had to do all the decision making and work to get here.
4. Relatedness – I still have my super strong wing people supporting me.
5. Status – I still have work coming in so I know I've not let the past few months affect this side of life too much.

I recognize that spending time, effort, and money on decorating may make the house feel more like mine, but I also know I'll likely continue to panic, and possibly more so, because it won't fundamentally change anything within me, it will only change the look and feel of the house.

Relatedness, along with Status is not triggered. At all. I don't need new pals and I have no desire to go out and join local groups. Groups are not a thing I particularly enjoy, and I don't feel socially isolated. It really takes a lot for me to feel 'left out' of anything so there is hardly ever any pain associated with this domain. So, I think, I need to focus on relatedness.

I decide I will immerse myself in things with new people. I will say yes to anything offered (within reason) and try anything new even if it doesn't sound like my kind of thing. Instead of worrying about the uncertainty of things and trying to put things in place to make things feel more 'normal' for me, I will focus on other things entirely. For three months I will throw myself at other people and say yes. To everything.

First, I join the local running group. They meet twice a week, are a sociable bunch, and often go for coffee after. It's a good start to meeting some people in the area and they convince me to sign up for a couple of local organized events.

Next, one of my new neighbours suggests outdoor swimming. On the inside I'm thinking 'not a chance' but I have to say yes and so a week later I find myself shivering on a loch side in my togs getting blasted with a cold spring wind and wondering 'why, why, why?' I tentatively put my big toe in the water and squeal loudly on the inside. A few minutes later I have taken the plunge and this time squeal loudly on the outside. It is so very painful. Everywhere aches from the cold. But then I notice an overwhelming sense of calm. The water laps quietly, there is mist rolling in the surrounding trees and hills, a wee fish jumps up just feet away and ducks with ducklings are paddling about contentedly. I feel like a huge weight has lifted. Something has shifted.

Ten minutes later and I'm shivering in the back seat of the car as we drive back home. I feel weirdly alive and full of energy and when offered the number of a local outdoor swim group I snap it up and text them to join before I can change my mind. The very next weekend finds me welcomed into this swim group that is instantly warm, supporting, and, I suspect full of people who will become lifelong friends. There is no pressure to go beyond what's comfortable, but there is shared laughter, pain, tea, and biscuits. And it's still only 8.30am in the morning.

Within just a few weeks I've met a lot of neighbours, gone dog walking with other dog owners, ran, for the first time with a running group, and become a regular loch 'douker'. As I drink coffee on the terrace one early summer morning, I notice how calm I feel. I reflect that this place is starting to feel like home. I've met enough people to feel like I can ask people for help, know that some new friendships have been initiated, and been blown away by the kindness and generosity I've received by just putting myself out there. The pain caused by the lack of certainty, autonomy, and fairness has died down to a much more manageable level. The house still looks exactly the same as the day after moving but no amount of redecoration would have had this level of impact. Things no longer feel so uncertain. By focusing on something else entirely, something I didn't feel I needed to put effort into at all, I have in fact significantly reduced the uncertainty that was panicking me so much.

A week later and I'm laughingly telling my friend who's visiting about my seemingly 'Hollywood' version of country living. We are sitting out having lunch, lunch of locally smoked fish from the fish van that visits once a week, salad from the local farms and picked up at the honesty box farm shop, and bread that is baked in the local village. Afterwards, we have freshly picked fruit (from a different farm shop) with fresh cream from the milkman. I wave to the postman as he yells over a greeting from afar. I then mention the lady I met in the woods recently who 'shoots pheasant at the weekend' and who, last week, left a couple for me at my back door. I have, I tell my friend, even managed to butcher them myself.

We finish lunch with coffee from a nearby coffee roasting company and watch three deer run through the field behind the house. I point out a red squirrel running up a tree and ask if they can hear the wood-pecker. It all seems too good to be true but is in fact the life that is unfolding. My friend jokes that all I need now is for a handsome woodcutter to knock on the door.

And then the doorbell rings. We both look at each other with wide eyes and I come back a few minutes later laughing. It was, I say, the joiner, but not, I say, quite the handsome woodcutter we both imagined. But it does leave a thought about that side of life, a thought I haven't, until now, had.

I spend the next few weeks being entirely busy with other people and other things, things I normally would have definitely said no to. I do things I perhaps won't do again but I enjoy the process of just saying yes. And the house, the thing I thought was so important to get it how I wanted? It still looks exactly the same as the day after I moved in, so much so that the pictures are all still in the wrong place, but it doesn't matter because it *feels* like home. My new home for my new life that is slowly unfolding. I reflect again, that by not focusing on the thing I thought would fix my social pain (uncertainty) and instead doing things for a non-triggered domain (relatedness) I have in fact removed the pain of uncertainty pretty much entirely. And I now know that everything I have done, despite the pain, grief, fear, and anxiety was absolutely the right decision.

And so, I decide, despite dementor protestations and without too much thought, to get a new puppy. Why not!

Chapter 14

Endings and beginnings

Monday 1st August[43]

I look back at the last six months. What a journey, I think. But I know that I have used my resources well. I minimized the dementors, especially when in a panic or when needing to make difficult decisions, I used many of my change management tools to help move me forward when I felt stuck, and I focused on how I physically felt to try and control my emotions and responses. Even if I couldn't fully control how I felt or reacted, I could, at least, reduce the impact by labelling how I felt and just accepting it when I needed to. I congratulate myself on getting to this point reasonably intact.

---

[43] Dates are mentioned in the next two chapters because *a lot* happens. The dates hopefully give you a sense of just how manic August was and how that can impact on our decisions.

It's time, I think, to just try and relax and start to really enjoy this new life. And I do. Until later that night. When I wake up in a panic.

The kind of panic where you're not sure why you're panicking but know there's something you've missed or forgotten. And then it hits me. I suddenly remembered the difficult thing I haven't done yet. And it's not insubstantial.

So, what is this mammoth task I've been putting off? Well, I haven't actually processed all the stuff. The emotional stuff. The ex-partner stuff. The 'being on my own' for the first time stuff. The stuff I decided to park while I threw myself into creating this new life. I realize I really need to process how I actually feel about the end of my relationship and what might come next out of that emotional hole.

Tuesday 2nd August

It's Jac day. The day my favourite person and most solid of rocks is visiting and I'm excited to show her around this amazing new place I've landed.

The morning is full of laughter, glee, and a wee bit of douking. On our way to the loch we pass through some ancient standing stones, stones I had decided were magical. Stones I had decided transported me into a pain-free universe every time I went for a swim. Stones that whenever I passed through caused me to cheer and feel alive and happy. I explain this to Jac, and she joins me in the loud 'whoo-hooo' as we drive through the middle of this ancient lay line of mystical stones. I know this is silly, but I also know it's a great brain hack. By attaching a positive story to something physical and repeating it over and over, you can, in just a short time, trigger the good feeling whenever you see or touch the thing.[44]

We've just had lunch when everything comes gushing out. The pent up, built up, ignored for several months' worth of emotions. I start to properly grieve for myself and the old life. And it feels cathartic. I'm not angry or bitter, and I feel like I can let some of the toughness go as my new home is, well, home and I feel safe and secure here. This feels like part of the healing process. I can start to really let go of the past, I think. I reflect how much easier this perhaps is by having removed all the reminders, all the things from my old life that were triggers of what I'd lost. In this moment I feel that I'm in a safe place and safe company to just let it all out. And I do.

---

[44] It's almost two years later now but whenever I go for a swim I still get a sense of euphoria as I pass through these stones.

Thursday 4th August

The tears are reducing, and today is also a very exciting day as we are heading into the city to see one of my favourite bands of all time, one I've never before seen live. I feel like an excited teenager as we arrive at the most perfect small outdoor venue on a very fine summers evening. I can't remember the last time I went on a proper night out.

The band come on the tiny stage, just a few metres from where we are sitting, and I start to feel a tad emotional (again) as they start playing an old favourite. I'm both laughing and crying at the same time as I realize it's ridiculous to be crying at a pretty heavy alternative rock band but who's watching, I think? 'Over there' Jac nudges me with her elbow and nods over to a very fine looking younger chap who is most definitely watching. I have no idea what to do or how to respond. It has been decades since I've been in this space and I honestly haven't even considered that I might, at some point, get back on that horse. I wouldn't even know where to start.

I suddenly feel alive and imagine I'm 16 again and we head into the mosh pit where we end up dancing and singing and laughing for two hours with a bunch of other fans including the previously mentioned younger man. It is exactly what I needed and I feel amazing, full of potential for what might be. I have so many new and raw feelings whizzing about, feelings I realize I have been subconsciously suppressing. I feel like a phoenix rising from the ashes. I feel invincible and realize I can do anything I want. There is nothing stopping or holding me back from a wealth of opportunities and it's time to grab life by the you-know-whats. It is probably one of the best and most defining nights of my life and I get to spend it with the most important person in my life.

Friday 5th August

After dropping Jac off at the station I decide to have a 'do nothing' afternoon on the terrace, thinking about all these new emotions and feelings and thoughts. Until now the thought of dating hasn't even entered my mind. Until now I was quite content getting used to being alone. I recall I always said I'd never internet date because it just seems so 'not me'. But suddenly I feel like I might want to see where these new feelings might take me and the chances of randomly meeting someone seem pretty slim. At least in the short term. I recognize that I'm barely out of a long-term relationship and I know that casual 'fun' is not me. I also know that I really don't have the time or energy for anything else in my life just now and really should focus on getting used to living alone. On top of all this, work has taken a backseat this year and really should, now that I'm feeling a bit more settled, be a priority, especially as this is also book launch month. But I can't shake these thoughts and feelings. And once I decide something then, as you may be aware by now, I really do move forward quickly. But this internet dating malarky sounds just terrible, demoralizing, full of rejection and disappointment and I know, could end up burning lots of time and energy. What to do?

Life ninja move 7

Story: We all tell ourselves stories and those stories become our reality. Therefore, the way you tell your story will impact and influence the reality you perceive. Think about all those excuses you make for 'not having time to...' You know if you really wanted to do the thing, mostly it's the gym or a run or something, then you would make the time, just like you make time for the things you really want to do, but the story is convenient and so you convince yourself it's true. Your mindset for any particular thing will impact your ability to do, or not do, the thing in question, and it's all based on the stories you have told yourself.

A good example is my dad who has struggled for years with technology. For him, it's still a newfangled thing and in his mind he's far too old to learn it. Whenever I try and show him how to fix something he refuses to listen properly or learn how to do it himself and so when the same thing happens again, he assumes there's something wrong with the phone or laptop and decides instead to replace it. On the couple of occasions he has tried to fix something he has failed, and this failure just confirms the story he's told himself that he's too old to learn this 'newfangled technology'.

Interestingly he's pretty good at woodwork, something he's learned to do in later life and something he practises until he gets it right. If it's not quite right he takes time to see where it went wrong and does it again, learning from his mistakes. He enjoys it and is motivated to get better, knowing that with practice and effort he will get closer to his goal.

 **Tool:** The stories you tell yourself about what you can and can't do is often called 'mindset', specifically growth and fixed mindset. If you tell yourself you can't do something because… Then if you try to do it and it doesn't work immediately then this confirms your thinking, that this thing is just impossible for you. However, if you set out to achieve a goal for something that motivates and excites you then if, nay when, you get things wrong you start to pay attention to what you need to work at or practice, until you get it right (like learning chords on the guitar or learning to serve at tennis). With this mindset you are much more open to failure because you know that with practice, and effort, you will get better, improve, and get closer to your goal.

My dad has a fixed mindset to technology because he thinks he's not smart enough to learn it but has a growth mindset to woodwork because he knows there's lots still to learn and the learning excites him. Your mindset is fluid and depends on the task at hand. But when you have a growth mindset you are much more likely to set aside time to 'practise or do' and to seek help and learn from others when you need it. When you have a fixed mindset, spending time practising something can feel like an utter waste of time because you've already told yourself you won't be able to achieve this goal anyway, and asking others for help only confirms this story further. The good, nay great, news is you can shift your mindset. And it really isn't that difficult.

You just need to retell your own story to yourself.

The easiest way to do this is to think about the attributes and factors that allow you to have a growth mindset and find a way to apply those attributes and factors to your fixed mindset challenge. So if my dad thought about how he learnt how to do a dove tail joint, by breaking it down into steps, checking the measurements, looking at it from different sides, taking small steps to see what might be wrong, and applied it to a feature on his phone or laptop to understand how that worked then he would, I have no doubt, improve his ability to fix basic technical issues. And once he's managed to do that first thing, he'll likely become motivated to learn the next thing because he will be telling himself a different story about his abilities.

Application: Think of something you are stuck on just now, maybe something you keep procrastinating over. Something you've told yourself is just impossible to do: You don't have the time; the knowledge; the skills; the talent; the motivation. It might be a course you should do, the 'Couch to 5k' you promised you would start, writing that book that's in you somewhere. What is the challenge?

Next think about all the attributes, behaviours, and reasons that are stopping you do it. What is the story you are telling yourself?

Now think about something you have done where you once had low ability and now would say you do reasonably well. Something where, despite the low ability at the start you: practised; learnt things; asked others for help; dedicated time to improve.

What did you do to enable you to improve and reach your goal? What attributes, behaviours, and actions allowed you to progress and succeed to a level you are happy with? Did you learn the piano, get a degree while working full time, learn a new language? What was the goal you set out to achieve and what made you continue, even when it might have all seemed too hard to do?

Now go back to the first challenge. The one you're stuck on. The one you've told yourself you just can't do. Then look at the things (attributes, behaviours, actions) you did in the second one, to achieve that goal. Next explore what you can draw from those things to help you take the first step toward the thing you are stuck on. What could you do that will start to shift you from a 'I can't do this because…' to 'I can't do this yet…'[45] but I will start with this simple small step of…'.

Insight: What insights have you had about the types of stories you tell yourself? Have you noticed a shift in your intention towards the goal you are procrastinating on? Have you had an 'a-ha' moment? Did you identify a small action you can do that will start you progressing towards the goal that you are procrastinating on?

Reflection: The aim here is not to get from A to Z but to get from A to B by changing the story you have told yourself about your own abilities, to shift you from a fixed mindset to a growth mindset for a particular goal. Understanding how to shift your mindset has huge implications when approaching new things, especially new things you keep procrastinating over and coming up with 'reasons' and excuses not to do them.

And remember, with a growth mindset, getting things wrong or failing just indicates where you need

---

[45] Adding the word yet to something opens up possibilities, for you and others. It can quickly shift a fixed mindset to growth.

to pay attention. When you have a growth mindset you are open to feedback to learn, improve, and to doing things differently.

 **Points time:** This can be a tough one to do, at least the first time, so grab 20 points for every new insight you've had that will help you shift your fixed mindset to a growth mindset.

Once you've done a small action towards the goal you are currently procrastinating on then come back and collect a bonus 40 points.

If, however you decide that you *never* have a fixed mindset then deduct 20 points from your overall score. This isn't a competition, and I would suggest if you think you *never* have a fixed mindset then perhaps you have a fixed mindset to thinking about mindsets!

Health points = _____

And so, what to do? I have all these feeling and emotions bubbling around that are pointing me to try dating. But I have all the reasons not to: It's too soon;

I'm too busy with other things (work and social); I'm only just processing the end of my relationship and still feeling pretty delicate; I'm pretty much against internet dating because it sounds horrific and demoralizing. *Pure Fixed Mindset* I tell myself. And there's no time like the present.

So, I reframe the story I'm telling myself. If I try internet dating I might meet new friends in my area, it could be fun, it could be entertaining, I will learn about what I want, and not want, from a future partner, and so on.

I dive in and sign up for a couple of dating apps.

Chapter 15

A Tinderella story

Saturday 6th August

I create a profile quickly and load up a recent photo where I just look like me on a daily basis. I have little expectation of anything happening, but I have made the first step.

I quickly learn the left and right swipe action which seems inhumane but gets easier with practice. I decide I really need to practise texting so am less scrutinizing of the profiles to increase my chances of matches.

And so, the world of internet dating reveals itself to me.

Why, I wonder, would someone post a picture of their car or motorbike? Why I wonder would someone put up a group picture and not say which one they are? Despite being very open to any old match, I still swipe left a lot.

And then the texting starts. The chap who says he is outgoing, active, and guaranteed to make me laugh and yet when I ask what he is up to for the weekend his response is 'watching tv'; the chap who is paranoid about actually going on a date because internet dating doesn't work; the chap who when asked how he's spending his day off responds with a particularly unsavoury image; the chap who's a comedy geek but unmatched me when I seem to have some knowledge of comedians; and the many, many chaps who ask not a single question and respond with one word answers to my questions. But it doesn't deter me. I'm a Change Ninja with a growth mindset.

After a couple of days of being entertained though I do acknowledge that this could easily become pretty depressing and demoralizing even though my expectations are low. But I do need to practise this 'dating thing', so onwards I shall go.[46] But first, I need to set some proper parameters because this could become all consuming of time and thought.

I sit down to think about how I should approach this. I start with my list of must-haves but quickly realize this is a new life and new me and these must-haves are from 30 years ago or they are things I enjoyed sharing with my ex-partner (like music). Is that really important to me now, I wonder, when it's no longer a significant part of my life? The list, I realize, is a list

---

[46] The last time I dated I was a gig going, Guinness guzzling, poverty-stricken student ready to take on the world.

that's trying to re-create what I've lost, or what I've chosen to leave behind. It's a list, I realize, of what would have served me well in my old life. So how should I go about building the parameters for dating for the new me and the new life when I don't really know what I'm looking for?

Life ninja move 8

Story: When you are looking to upgrade, swap, replace, revamp, restart, or make big changes it can be hard to know what might work because it's going to be, well, new.

The temptation might be to think about what worked last time, list all the good things about the last one and then add all the new things you now want before going out in search of your new house, job, sofa, car, or spouse.

But what served you well in the past may no longer serve you now for the new you. That is why you are looking to change. And if you create such a list then it's possible you will miss opportunities for exploring things you haven't yet considered.

The challenge is that your brain likes the familiar and fills in the gaps with what it already knows. Even if something is not right for you, it can't fill in gaps with new things that might be good for you because it can't imagine completely new experiences. The brain can only work with the information it already has. So, if you really do want 'new' then you need fresh eyes to get new insights about what that 'new' could look like.

Tool: The FiveEyes™ are five different lenses to look through in order to gain fresh insights about what might work well for you.

1. **Slow-mo-eye** – Think about an experience you've had recently, like a date you maybe went on, and look at it again but at a slower pace. This allows you to see things that you might have missed at regular speed. It gives you the space to detach yourself a little from the experience, like a cat watching a fishbowl. What do you see as you slow it down? What does the experience look like now? What's happening that you missed the first time?

2. **Instant replay eye** – This time look at what you are looking at several times to see all of the detail. For example, on a dating profile you might make a quick judgement based on a description or a photo. But if you have another look you might see what else is going on. Read the profile again, is it odd or is there hidden humour in it? Look at

the background in the photo. What else can you glean from the information that you might not see straight away. Is the ill-fitted suit or wonky tie a sign of bad dressing or a sign of a rebel not wanting to wear a tie at all? Does the 'great outdoors loving' description match the pictures, or does it look like all they do is sit in bars drinking? Does the slightly over preened picture suggest arrogance or confidence?

3. **Magnif-eye** – Identify something that is important for you and then blow it up in your mind for a better look. This is a great one for creating your real must-haves for something new. And I mean *must-haves*. A good example is when I started texting potential dates, I had a way of finding out what type of music they were interested in and would change my views of them if it was music I didn't like. But when I magnified this up, and really looked into it I realized that this was important to me 30 years ago. Now? Music is a tiny part of my life, and I have gig-going pals for the odd gig I do go to. When I blew this requirement up, I realized music was a ridiculous thing to think of as important for me in this new life. Ask yourself, does someone really need to be 6'2, does the new house really need three bathrooms, or does the new job really need to be in the public sector? Magnif-eye helps you work out what really is important for you right now.

4. **Filmstrip eye** – Imagine you've just had the perfect date, seen the perfect job, or perfect house. You get excited thinking this could bode well for the future. This could be the one! Before you get too excited, think about what you had to do in advance to make it to this point. And think about what else was done in advance to get to this point, possibly by someone else – like your potential new boss. If you're on a date and your date knows all the Wes Anderson films, something you've told them you really enjoyed. Is it a match made in heaven or might something else be true? Have they perhaps swotted up in advance? Now think what might happen next and how the future will unfold if it turns out they've never seen a Wes Anderson film and have no interest in doing so? Think about that perfect hybrid job that they say has flexible working patterns. How do you think it will go if you tell them you want to work from home all the time after doing the hybrid commute for three weeks? How will your next date go if you don't have the 30 minutes to wash your hair in advance and need to turn up in your dog walking clothes? Play out the film before and after to see what small things you might be dismissing as unimportant might suddenly become game changers.

5. **Why-eye** – Something happens, it doesn't feel right, and you are ready to respond, put up the barriers, fight back. But pause and think about

what is causing what you are experiencing. Has your new potential boss not sent the information they promised? Do you think they've changed their mind and start to write an email to double check? Do you think they don't really care and it's making you wonder if this is the right move after all? Have you sent a joke text to your potential date and they've not responded? Do you think they've changed their mind or thought you were being serious and you decide to send an explanation text to clear things up? Before you do anything stop and think 'what assumptions am I making?' Mis-perceived assumptions about behaviours can lead to a quick exit. The new boss might, for example, have been called into an emergency meeting. The new date might, for example, be in a work meeting. We often respond quickly to things based on our potential misinterpretations rather than taking time to think 'what else might be true?'

 Application: Pick out a new thing you want to look at in your life, something that requires change. Dating, job, house, car, sofa, something to fill in empty nest syndrome. Anything to get you started with this tool.

Now pick a lens and apply it to what you have imagined this new thing will look or be like.

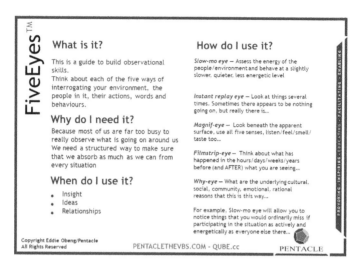

What is holding true for you in this new thing? What assumptions, past needs, or past behaviours are you clinging onto because they are familiar but perhaps will no longer serve you well?

Write down your new criteria and real must-haves. Also write down the things you perhaps need to let go, the things that once served you well and feel are important but in fact no longer serve you well at all.

Insight: What have you discovered? What have you now dismissed that before seemed incredibly important? What new things do you now realize are important that you hadn't even thought about? What are you keeping open to allow you to explore opportunities you can't yet imagine?

Reflection: The FiveEyes™ is a really good tool to think about things from very different perspectives. You develop behaviours, and your conscious personality, often from social and personal pressures at particular points in life. Things that worked well for you in the past may therefore no longer work well for you in the now and in the new future you are imagining. But remember the brain likes to save energy and automate as much as possible so it will always jump to the familiar and safe unless you intervene. These five different lenses will give you a different perspective to help decide what you might need to get rid of, and what new habits and behaviours you need to create to reflect who you want to be and what you really want from the change you are going through.

Points time: For each new insight, a thing you didn't know was important, or a thing you no longer think is important gain 20 points.

Health points = _____

I sit down to look at each of the FiveEyes™ and wonder how I will apply them to dating. This, I think, will help my success rates in finding reasonable matches rather than matching to nutters, red herrings, and time wasters. This will in turn reduce the amount of physical and emotional energy I spend on this bit of my life.

Once I've been through each of the FiveEyes™ I write down my rules for dating.

TAM'S RULES FOR DATING

1. I will only ever be who I am. No pretending or exaggerating. This means being vulnerable when it feels safe to be or taking a sharp exit if I don't think I can be me. It must feel right in my gut. *Slow-mo-eye*.

2. I will not focus too much on photos/looks. They can be deceiving, and I know that real connections happen based on much more than physical looks and connections change how you see a person anyway. *Instant replay eye*.

3. I list my real non-negotiable must haves. Things that further down the line could cause issues if they aren't met:
   a) Must like dogs (and demonstrate they actually do rather than just say it).

---

b) Must look after themselves physically. They don't need to be super fit gym bunnies, it's more about self care and self respect.

c) Must eat well. I'm not looking for perfect, but food, cooking, and diet are very important to me.

It's not, I think, a tall ask. Other things I think are important can probably be compromised on if necessary. *Magnif-eye.*

4. Using the *Why-eye* I list my definite instant no-no's:[47]
   a) Selfies taken in the gym.
   b) Photos of a car/motorbike.
   c) Hobbies listed as Netflix, cocktails, and takeaways.

5. Each new connection will be treated as practice, and I will use the feedback to learn more about what I might actually be looking for. I need to practise:
   a) Messaging.
   b) Video calls.
   c) Dating.

---

[47] Don't @me. I have my reasons!

After each experience I will use the *slow-mo-eye* and *film-strip-eye* to see what fresh insights this might bring before committing to the next step.

6. I accept that while humour is incredibly important to me, I pretty much can turn any situation into a funny one, I also know that humour between people, the kind that matters in a close relationship, might not be instant and might take time to develop. The *Why-eye* will be invaluable to check things are aligning like humour and core values and will stop me turning someone away because they don't instantly make me guffaw.
7. I really do need to trust my gut. If it doesn't feel right don't persuade myself that it might be OK. There should be zero self-negotiation and just common (gut) sense. See rule 1.
8. It's 'them not me' will be my mantra. Other people's actions and behaviours are nothing to do with me. But they might make a good, nay funny, story one day.

I reflect that the FiveEyes™ has really helped me look at things differently which is exactly what I needed. And while I acknowledge this might be another emotional rollercoaster, I do, by now, know how to check in on how I'm feeling.

I'm ready. Let the dating begin in earnest.

And so, I start again, sign up to another app and apply Tam's rules for dating. This time I've lowered the age range. Who says it needs to be someone the same age or older? That's old school thinking. Pretty soon I get matches from some very handsome younger chaps who are clearly on Tinder for its original purpose and use openers such as 'hello beautiful'. They are quickly deleted. If I'm going to do this then I'm going to do it properly and casual flings are not my style at all. I start to have some amusing banter with someone who looks like an excellent match but on asking what he's up to he tells me he's 'lying in bed watching porn'. Delete. Another is extremely keen to get off the dating app and to have me over for dinner and complains when I won't give him my phone number. Delete. And then just a range of what initially seem like normal guys but who quickly verge into the 'creepy' territory. I spend little time with these people and am quick to: Delete. Delete. Delete.

I limit myself on the app but with my pre-agreed criteria find I can whizz through a lot of profiles quickly. If I get a match I go back and look at the profile using the FiveEyes™, before deciding whether or not to make contact.

My neighbour pops over for coffee. As I tell her what I'm up to she gets concerned about my safety. I explain my rules and that, by applying them, I have pretty much eliminated about 99.5% of potential matches.

'This means the chances of ending up matching to a serial killer are pretty slim', I say. 'So on the very, very tiny chance I do end up dating a serial killer I will, at least, know they are pretty smart and creative to have got past my rules.'

This seems to relax her somewhat.

Wednesday 10th August

I get a nice match, the rules are all checked and we start to text. On Thursday we've shared quite a bit of information and agree a meet up on Sunday. OK, so I accept I've gone from texting to date without the video bit, but they are pretty local and some rules are ok to break occasionally.

We continue texting on Friday but then a few texts in the evening are unanswered despite saying we would chat after dinner. What else might be true I think (*Why-eye*) and give them the benefit of the doubt. Saturday is the same and on Sunday I accept they've checked out. I've been ghosted. For my first potential date. How *rude* I think. What is wrong with people? What is wrong with sending a polite sorry I've changed my mind? They don't even un-match me. But I find humour in the situation by thinking 'seriously, ghosted at my age?', and remember the mantra, 'It's them, not me'.

Monday 15th August

I have some great chat with a few other folk, but circumstances and locations don't lend themselves to taking things further. It's not a waste of time as the situations prove to be good practice, they improve my confidence, and help me realize there are people out there I seem to connect with quite easily, at least at a level that is helping me to explore this new venture. I'm feeling pretty perky about it all. Then I have another potentially good match from someone who seems a bit keener than me and after a few messages, suggests a video chat that evening. And while I'm not utterly convinced (gut feel), there is no threat if it goes wrong and rule 5 says I need to practise and haven't yet had a video meet up. What could go wrong?

It's time for the call and I feel a little nervous. I meet new people virtually all the time for work, but this feels different. My phone starts to ring and I accept the call. A face appears on the screen looking pretty dishevelled, pretty unlike their profile picture and as soon as they say 'hello', I notice a pretty major problem. They have no teeth and appear to be gurning at me. I know I said looks shouldn't be important initially, but they have misled me slightly. It makes me think that they don't really look after themselves (bridges and caps are available from all good dentists). My brain is frantically trying to work out how I might get out of this call without seeming rude (even for a practice run this isn't going to work) when he lets me know his Wi-Fi is a bit ropey and he needs to go and have a word with 'the lad on his Xbox'. He'll call me back in five he says.

I never hear from him again. Mr Gurney Gurner has had one look at my video face and dumped me! There is nothing to do but find humour in this as well. It is so ridiculous that I don't even need my mantra of 'It's them and not me'.

Wednesday 17th August

Someone fairly local matches and I respond positively. Their profile is incredibly well aligned to mine, similar age, jobs, not too far away, similar hobbies, and they appear to have all of the must haves and none of the must have nots. We quickly get into full text conversations over the next couple of days before arranging to meet on Saturday. This I think, could actually be my first real date. I'm pretty confident there will be no ghosting here. I'm even comfortable with the fact that they really don't like my type of music!

Saturday 20th August

I'm wracked with nerves. Confident me is all of a wobble. This year has been nothing *but* meeting new people, but this feels very different. I haven't been on a date for nearly 30 years. It is a very weird feeling. We are meeting at the beach and I'm taking the dogs (rule 3 must have). If it's terrible I can also use them as an excuse to leave early.

I park the car and go to let the dogs out the boot. My date has spotted me and is heading over. There is the initial clumsy handshake, cheek kiss, and I grab the dogs leads. I notice that they haven't greeted the dogs. We head down to the beach, it's a beautiful day, blue skies, a slight breeze but nice and warm and the conversation flows pretty easily. But again, I notice that they don't pay any attention to the dogs. They're just not interested in them. *At all.* We end the date with a cup of tea before I suggest I'd best get back as the dogs would be getting hungry. The date ends on a positive and as I'm driving home I think about a second date. But as soon as I'm home I quickly check my list and remember if they don't have the three must haves then it's a 'must not' from me. If someone is in my life then the dogs are part of that life and liking dogs isn't the same as wanting dogs and accepting that the dogs might get in the way sometimes. The rules were made to avoid any emotional upset and to avoid wasting time on the wrong people and getting demotivated by it all.

I send them a follow up text thanking them for nice afternoon but that I don't want to pursue a second date. No ghosting!

Sunday 21st August

I'm sitting eating dinner at the dining table. This is something I've forced myself to do every night. No dinner in front of the TV and ideally no dinner with my phone either. This evening I'm reading my book but it's a virtual book on my tablet and so notifications do pop up as I'm reading. I mostly ignore them, but a wee note pops up saying someone has matched and messaged me. I don't expect it to be anything of real interest, but we are programmed to peek at these things and it is incredibly hard it is to resist once we know a message is there. And so, I take a peek and instantly think 'hello' as I flick through a bunch of photos of a nice, handsome young chap, up in the hills. My first thought is to wonder why he's texting me, but we enter into conversation that's light hearted and funny and seems pretty open.

As we continue to message, I head through to the lounge and what follows is a few hours of very healthy banter. It jumps around from humour, to sharing information about ourselves, to being open and a little bit vulnerable to being flirty (I find myself blushing a lot!). Mostly it just feels good and flattering, and while I'm naturally sceptical that it can't be this easy, I'm also thinking why not, why can't it? We seem to be moving things forward quite quickly. Neither of us are up for starting a long-term relationship but neither of us want casual either. We are however, both after some nice company, fun, and someone to do those couple of things with, without all the big strings and pressure of wondering where a relationship might go. And as the evening wears on we come up with a crazy plan to enter into a short-term relationship that has some up-front rules. Rules that will ensure maximum fun and zero stress of a long-term relationship. It won't matter, we decide, if we're not a perfect match. We'll just agree to see where we are at the end of March and then potentially call it day. It will have served its purpose for us both, we know we make each other laugh and have enough in common to get along and if we want to continue, we can but there will be no expectations to do so. No pressure. It sounds both ridiculous and ideal. It sounds like something I would never have even entertained or thought myself capable of six months ago. But this is the new me and I need to try new things.

At about 2am we decide that we'll bunk off work the next day to begin this crazy experiment. What could go wrong?

I turn out the lights and try to sleep but there is so much (good) adrenalin and dopamine zipping about my body by this point. This is a massive stretch for me, and completely out of my comfort zone but it's time to try something new. This year is all about 'new' and taking more (calculated) risk. And, of course, I'm still saying yes to everything.

Oh, it's probably worth mentioning here that there is another reason I'm a bit hyper at this point. Tomorrow morning brings with it another life-changing event. It's something for which I need to watch and wait to see what happens, but it is possibly one of *the* most exciting days of my life. Tomorrow is the launch day for *The Change Ninja Handbook*.[48] Possibly one of *the* biggest goals I've ever set out to

---

[48] Available from all good bookshops and a perfect prequel to this book.

achieve. Ever. That's sort of adding to the cocktail mix of 'feelings and emotions', which, while I don't recognize it right now, is really a stress response to what is going on, even though the 'going on' is a good thing. My brain is doing its job pointing me to an error signal – an error signal that I am duly ignoring.

Monday 22nd August

I get up from my non-slumber feeling anxious, nervous, excited, dry mouthed, and with zero appetite, so I make an extra large coffee before doing the final bits for book launch day. All I can really do then is sit and wait and see if it starts to sell (I have a cunning plan to get the book into the charts).

I then get ready for my date, which, based on our chat, is definitely more than just a regular first date. I spend a silly amount of time wondering what to wear before just throwing on a pair of jeans and a nice jumper. We will be taking the dogs out, drinking coffee, and seeing what happens.

At the allotted time I head to the park we are meeting in and as I sit in the car waiting, ask myself not for the first time 'what I'm doing?' This is, I know, not a regular date. We have, I know, already agreed the 'what next?' after the date *irrelevant* of how it goes because we accept it can take a couple of meet ups to get rid of the weirdness. We have been continuously texting all morning and we are both on the same page. As I wait, I decide to look at the Amazon book charts with little expectation of anything showing. I almost scream out loud. Well, there is no almost about it, I actually do scream out loud. Next to my book is the much sought after #1 best seller tag. Me, I laugh, a #1 best seller. I laugh and laugh and laugh some more. This is, I think, going to be a very fine day indeed.

My date arrives. We are both a little nervous, but the chat is good and we reconfirm our plan and tell ourselves it is perfect and really could work. And the date continues to progress well. Until, that is, the reality kicks in (for him), and the panic sets in (for him), and it all of a sudden (for him) seems like a completely crazy idea. Well not just for him, it seems crazy to me too but I'm happy to keep going. I possibly don't behave quite as well as I could, and it is ever so slightly possible that I sort of make a bit of an idiot of myself. OK, I definitely do make an idiot of myself and it is more than a bit. Things end a little odd with a 'let's talk later'. Once I've calmed down a little (it takes a while) I apologize for how I responded and we agree that we will chat again in a couple of weeks as he's off on holiday at the end of the week.

Chapter 16

Sami's[49] fables

Tuesday 23rd August

I feel exhausted. I have that post anticipation slump like you get after an exam that you worked really hard for. You do the exam well (you think), but then afterwards, once the relief of it being over passes, you just feel a bit flat. The date thing seems to have gone pear-shaped and while the book launch has gone amazingly well, I don't have anyone to share it with. Not properly.

I start to beat myself up a bit. I went a bit *off piste* on this one and it's come back to bite me. My imagined next best seller book 'Three weeks on Tinder' or 'How I beat Tinder' was, I accept, the fantasies of a slightly deranged middle-aged lady. But I honestly and truly believed, for a very brief moment, that I'd cracked this

---

[49] Sami is the wise old bean in *The Change Ninja Handbook*. This chapter is about creating your own 'learning' fables just like Aesop and Sami.

internet dating lark. The stress hormones are still doing their thing, but all the excitement is gone. Combined with the potential 'embarrassment' of how I behaved. I'm both physically and mentally exhausted.

But I know that if I learn from this it won't have been a waste of time and I also know that I can choose how I tell this story. Will it be embarrassing, shameful, or just a funny story of how this normally rational and logical person went ever so slightly off the rails and turned into a crazy lady.

Life ninja move 9

Story: When was the last time you wished – oh how you wished – you hadn't said or done that thing, hadn't acted in that way? What did you do after? Did you bury your head under the duvet? Did you stick your fingers in your ears and pretended none of it was happening? Did you beat yourself up over and over again? Do you still carry the shame, embarrassment, and mortification? Or did you learn from getting it wrong?

 **Tool:** We are all human and we all get things wrong. The easiest thing in the world would be to brush things under the carpet, but I know and you know that in reality you can mostly only pretend to do this. In reality the thing you are trying to ignore can quite easily start to eat away on the inside becoming a much bigger beast than it really is. However, if you learn from the thing you did that you're quietly cringing about, then it's unlikely you will make the same mistake again. And if you learn from it, you will probably, at some point, also be quite glad it happened because something good will come from the learning, like something good comes from all fables.

The key to learning as you go is to do just that. Learn as you go.

The best way to learn as you go is to do something called an ActionReplay™.

- What did you plan to do that worked well?
- What did you plan to do that didn't work well?
- What went wrong that you hadn't planned on doing?
- What went well that you hadn't planned on doing?

Application: Think of something you've done recently that's making you cringe a little on the inside, something you wish you'd handled differently.

Work through the four questions capturing as much information as you can.

Next, for each of the things you captured think about an action point. What might you do differently next time to avoid making the same mistake? And what might you do more of, the things that did work well?

Looking at the completed tool, if you start top left and work clockwise you will finish on the 'not planned and worked well' question, and this one *always* makes you feel good.

Insight: How do you feel about the thing you've reviewed. If it was something you maybe got wrong do you feel more empowered to do it much better next time? Has it removed some of the self-doubt and possible shame?

Reflection: When things go wrong, we can beat ourselves up. The story we tell ourselves about it can become shameful and embarrassing. It might stop us trying again.

Shame and failure are like a darkness. If you shine a light on them they disappear. If you own it, tell the story to others, add humour, learn from it, and do it differently next time, then the shame and sense of failure will, most definitely, disappear.

We're all human and we all make mistakes. But it's only a failing if you choose not to learn from it.

Points time: 20 points for each learning point that has an action assigned.

Health points = _____

I complete my ActionReplay™ on what just happened. There are a lot of learning points for me. I strayed from my rules. I behaved, for me, unacceptably. I still feel a bit of an idiot but I'm starting to find it funny. The combination of everything going on at the time meant I wasn't really being 'logical me' and I got a little carried away, which when it didn't work out, caused me to react badly. I really wasn't in a good emotional place to be making such big moves. I know there is no value in beating myself up, but there is value in learning. Maybe, I think, it's time, in life, to actually just calm down and get used to this new life before really working on the big 'what next?'.

Chapter 17

Once upon a time

Friday 26th August

So much for calming down, I think as I pack my rucksack. I have another 'had to say yes to' thing on this weekend. I'm off on a campervan weekend to one of the Scottish Islands with a new pal, her pal, and three dogs. While it's not great timing it should, I think, at least be fun. Not great timing because I'm still slightly distracted, nay wired, by all that has happened recently and all that is coming up. The all-out stress (good and bad) hormone attacks on my body of late is taking its toll, I'm physically whacked and am barely eating. On top of the weekend away which should be fun, if not exactly relaxing, I also have a busy week ahead including a virtual book launch on Thursday and an actual party at the house with all my new neighbours and friends, to celebrate the book, the move, and their friendship, on Friday.

As I throw my running gear into a separate bag (part of the reason for the trip is a local race) I hear the beep of my friend arriving to go and pick up the campervan.

Monday 29th August

I'm finally home and sitting having a cup of tea and asking myself, about every three seconds, 'Blimey, how did that happen?'.

The weekend was an utter disaster. It ended up with me doing pretty much all the driving, a trip that took 12 hours door to door. Given how wired I was this didn't feel safe. As a threesome we didn't really gel, and to make matters worse they decided it was too cold to camp (the original plan) and decided they'd join me in the van instead. Three adults and three dogs in essentially a pimped up white van did not make for the best of times. And it was pretty much downhill from there.

But brakes on, I think. I don't do the 'woe is me' story telling. I quickly focus on the positives and the humour and learning. I met an incredibly nice local chap on the ferry with whom I exchanged numbers and who ended up being my salvation. We didn't get to meet up unfortunately, but we did text constantly with me providing a running dialogue of events as they unfolded. Him finding the whole thing hilarious helped me realize that it wasn't me, it was them. The race we did, which was the main purpose of the trip, was simply delightful, local, small, beautiful scenery, and I won a medal.[50] I also managed to sneak off by myself for some of the best seafood I've ever eaten, met some great people,[51] and sold a couple of books. Overall, I had a lovely experience doing some firsts (campervan and the Hebrides). I know, by now, it's all in the stories we tell ourselves. It's all in the narrative. If we tell the stories in a positive, funny, way, to ourselves then the memories, feelings, and emotions will also be positive and funny when we remember them.[52]

Life ninja move 10

Story: Have you ever watched a film and been on the edge of your seat? Perhaps a pillow in front of your face to block out the frightening part? Or had tears flowing when a character dies in a tragic accident? This is good story telling. It may be something that's on the screen in front of

---

[50] OK, so it's likely I was the *only* one in my category but... a win is a win.
[51] Who I'm still in touch with.
[52] Remembering some of the specific moments on this trip still has me howling with laughter.

you – a fictional story – and yet you are feeling the emotions as if it's real. And if you later recall this film, perhaps you might tell someone else about how good it was and why, then you will probably notice that you feel the same emotions again as you talk through the plot. Emotions about something that wasn't even real!

 **Tool:** Story telling is such a powerful tool because you have the power to change the emotions that go with the story. When things happen in the real world, your brain 'perceives' what's going on and creates your reality and everyone has a different perception of reality based on their own personal experiences.

For example, as you watch a horror film, the lighting may change, the music may change, or the actor may look fearful. Your brain predicts that a terrifying thing is about to happen because it recognizes (from past horror films) what is going to happen next (something jumping out) which is what puts you on the edge of your seat and gets you ready to jump. When you do jump you might scream, or, in my case, you might laugh. Your emotional response will depend on the emotions you previously attached to this particular scenario. This is good news because this means you have control over the emotions you feel about scenarios, because emotions are just the story attached to what your brain is perceiving.

Another example. Imagine slipping over in the street and spilling your drink all over you. Do you feel embarrassed? Probably yes. But embarrassment is the emotion we've culturally learnt to attach to this scenario. It's unlikely you've ever seen a baby fall over and feel embarrassed. A baby is more likely to cry from the pain and shock, laugh, or just get up and carry on because they haven't yet learnt to attach the emotion of embarrassment to it. In fact, if they laugh and you laugh with them, they are much more likely to attach the emotion of humour to the fall next time it happens, assuming it doesn't hurt.

The more you tell a story, the stronger the emotion feels that you've attached to the story. If you feel embarrassed by something but choose to tell it as a funny story and tell it again and again as a funny story, the memory you have of the incident in future years is more likely to be a funny one.

 Application: Think of something you've done recently that didn't quite go to plan. Maybe it's something you're a bit annoyed about. Now try and tell the story in a different way. Try some of these suggestions:

1. Write or tell it as a sad story.
2. Write it tell it from someone else's perspective or in the third person.
3. Write it in an upbeat 'jolly hockey sticks', 'stiff upper lip' kind of way.

4. Write it as a comedy. I often think of a favourite comedian and tell it in their voice. Dawn French or Jenny Éclair are particularly good at self-deprecating humour.

Now tell the funny version to someone else. Then tell it again, and again.

 Insight: Did your emotions shift when you told the story in different ways. Are you looking back and able to chuckle to yourself about that 'embarrassing' incident? What have you noticed about your feelings, both the physical and emotional? How could you use this in future?

 Reflection: You can change how you *feel* about many situations because the emotion you attach to the situation is based on the story you are telling yourself. The story itself isn't reality but your interpretation of reality. The trick is remembering the brain will do the least effort and decide super quick what your interpretation of any situation is based on past experience and knowledge. Your challenge is to notice the physical feelings and the emotions, try and ignore what the brain is telling you and instead decide you're going to interpret this situation in a different way. If you do this often, you will create a new version of your reality, one that is, perhaps, a little easier to accept.

Points time: 20 life points for each story you rewrite or retell.

20 extra points if you've retold a negative story and are now laughing like a loon.

Health points = _____

Tuesday 30th August

I wake up late the next day after a very good night's sleep, the first in weeks. The curtains are open and once again I admire the view from my window while reflecting on the last few weeks and how blooming wild it has been. Just over three weeks ago Jac visited, and I finally had an emotional outburst and started to process what had happened to me this year. This prodded me into exploring the world of internet dating, where I had some fun chatting, was ghosted (twice), had one regular date, and got close to the point of having the start of some sort of relationship.

I've also had the (now funny) weekend away in a van and launched my first book. No wonder I'm exhausted, I reflect. Even though it has been mostly good things it's been too much, like a kid going to birthday parties every day for a week and being allowed to eat all the blue Smarties. I really should, I think, focus on the book, and me, as I'm pretty sure my body is going to rebel at some point and decide it needs some proper R&R. And while I know this is the right thing to do, I'm also still curious about the dating side so decide to have just one more wee look at Tinder, make a couple more swipes right and close the app. If nothing happens with these couple of swipes, then I'll delete the app, not for good, but for now. I look at my watch, have a minor panic, and get up. There is a lot still to do for the book launch and house party.

It's later that evening. I'm sitting out having a cold drink on the terrace before dinner when I get a notification flash on my phone. A swipe from earlier has resulted in a match and the chap has sent a message. We fall into easy conversation, he's fairly local, and on paper we match well based on jobs, age, interests, etc, but I'm more wary, applying my rules and the FiveEyes™ and not getting too excited.

On Wednesday we make plans to meet in a couple of weeks once we both have a bit more time. By Thursday we are having pretty in-depth conversations that continue over the weekend. By Monday I realize I might have met someone that might get me, and I delete the dating app. Due to unforeseen circumstances our actual meeting up is put on hold for a few weeks, but we text chat a lot. We discuss doing a video call as that would be most logical, but both think it will be awkward and we would rather wait until the opportunity presents to physically meet.

Over the next few weeks, we get to know each other pretty well. Warts and all. It's a very safe space and all the rules I made are being followed (see, I did learn from the previous 'going *off piste*' experience). I definitely feel like I'm getting to know this person and we seem to be connecting very well. Everyone tells me to be careful. Some even think this is a scam because we haven't met up yet. But we both reflect that this back to front way of getting to know each other, purely through text chat, has removed a lot of the initial awkward getting to know each other phase. That when you start off physically it's much harder to get past the politeness and the shyness. It's much harder to dig into the real stuff of 'what matters to me', much harder to get past the superficial. For us both, I think, it feels like we're at the three month kind of point, even though we have yet to meet.

And then we finally do meet. I'm nervous, excited, and scared because this has gone so very well, and I have placed quite a lot of hope in it. It can't be this easy I think, remembering my last experience. It just can't.

And so, we meet. And as predicted it all goes horribly, horribly wrong.

Only kidding. I know this is a real-life story and not a Hollywood romance film but it does go incredibly well. Beyond the first 15 minutes of getting used to each other's face and voice it feels very natural. All my worries and doubts disappear. Apart from one small niggling doubt. I hadn't, I realized, really contemplated meeting someone for a proper full-on relationship. Was I ready for this? I quickly eliminate this doubt because it just feels right and I feel, deep down, that this is going to work out.

And it does. The '21 days on Tinder' story I imagined in the middle of August, might be more like 24 days on Tinder but I do, after all, have my very own Tinderella story.

October arrives and we go on lots of nice walks and trips out with the dogs. I go on a short overseas trip with my nephew and laugh like a loon for four days. I realize I have a feeling of relief, that the hard stuff is over, I can finally breathe, relax, and enjoy things without any tinges of anxiety or fear or grief.

And that's when my body decides to pack up. It has served me very well in the last ten months but now needs some recovery time. I get a range of illnesses, nothing serious, but all at the same time and feel awful. I give into it. There's not much else I can do. And my new life rallies round and supports me in all the ways I need. My body has been in fight response for such a long time and even though I managed things pretty well by using all of my Change Ninja skills it was often a close call. So now I needed to physically recover and really start to enjoy the new life I'd created.

Chapter 18

Ninjaing Christmas

It's early in November and my neighbour knocks on the door and randomly asks if I want anything from the chippy. I am still saying yes to everything. Why stop when it has worked out so very well so far? And so, despite the chippy not being my kind of thing I ask for a battered haddock and say I'll warm up some plates and open a bottle of wine.

'Would you like to join me?' I ask. He doesn't take long to say yes!

As we are finishing our supper we start to talk about Christmas. I hadn't, until this point even thought about it, and it suddenly dawns on me that I might be 'home alone'. Without pause or hesitation I find myself inviting my neighbour and his parents to join me. He doesn't take long to say yes!

An hour later and I start to do the dishes when my phone pings. It's a text message from my cousin. 'We were wondering if we could come up for Christmas?' she asks. This time *I* don't take long to say yes!

And while I still have the warm cheery glow of wine and good cheer about me, I decide to invite my other new (but now ex) neighbours to join us as they've been lifesavers over the summer. With, of course, their two giant beasts of dogs. I'll worry, nay panic, about it later.

Christmas approaches. I now have eight guests across five households, including my new chap and four dogs to contend with. Most of the guests don't really know each other and out of the eight I only really know my cousin well. Everyone else is pretty new to me. So much for taking it easy for a while I think to myself, not for the first time.

But if this year has taught me something it is that I am most definitely a Change Ninja. This will, I think, after this year's events, be easy-peasy, lemonade squeezy. My first Change Ninja action, I think, is to get out the stun gun and kill me some aliens, which is what I call risks.

Life ninja move 11

Story: I'm guessing at some point you have watched an alien film. Spoiler alert if you haven't because they all follow the same formula.

First an alien appears on the spaceship hurtling through space and the crew assume it's evil and so they send out a small search party to kill it. The small search party head off and determine it would be a good idea to 'split up' resulting in one of them being eaten. *Crew 0 – Alien 1.*

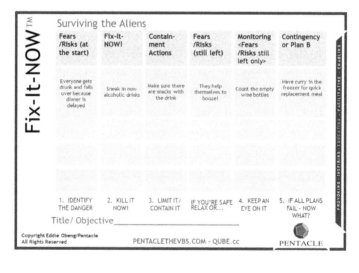

Next, they send out the A-team of search parties with bigger guns. The A-team manage to capture the alien, high five each other, lock it up for further investigation, and decide a cold beer is needed. The alien escapes. *Crew 0 – Alien 2.*

The alien gets lonely so has lots of baby aliens in a bid to take over the ship. The crew try to monitor where the aliens are but find that they are slowly getting eaten, one by one, in their bid to kill all the alien babies. *Crew 0 – Alien 3.*

Once they are down to only one crew member, plan B is enacted which is blow up the spaceship. *Crew 0 – Alien 4* (the alien wins because there is always a sequel!)

This is not, I repeat not, *how* to manage risk but does provide the formula *how to* manage risk.

Tool: Follow these simple steps to annihilate your aliens:

1. Identify your key risks. If you think of them as aliens that might eat you it's much easier.
2. Then think 'How can I kill this risk dead?' Top tip – don't split up!
3. If trying to kill it dead doesn't work, how will you contain it? Top tip – don't get distracted and allow it to escape.
4. Once you've done all of that, what risk/fear might still be left?
5. How could you monitor the risk that's left? Top tip – where are all the baby aliens?

6. Finally, what is your Plan B? How will you blow up the spaceship to stop maximum disruption and aliens taking over the world or in this case fears coming true?

7. Ideally you will kill the risk dead, but thinking through each step will mean you don't repeat the same mistakes they do in the films because you will have a cunning plan ready for all the things that *could* happen to derail your project.

 Application: Have a go at doing this just now. What is going on in your life just now that might have some 'risk' attached?

Start by writing down what the alien is. Then just to make sure it is the problem that needs killing ask you self why is this an alien? What's the 'so what?' if it happens? Keep digging until you have the real risk you need to kill. When you do this, you have much better chance of killing it dead.

For example: I might think I have a risk that dinner will be late because it takes too long to prepare. I might think I'll kill this risk by starting the preparation the day before or getting up at 4am. None of that pleases me. But if I ask what the 'so what?' of dinner being late is I find that the real risk is that people get drunk quickly because they have empty tummies which means possible fighting or falling over. This may of course also happen even if food is served on time. So, the real 'so what' risk is drunkenness. This is my alien:

- I can **kill** the alien dead by sneaking in non-alcoholic fizz every other bottle!
- I can **contain** the risk by providing snacks with the drinks.
- I can **monitor** any left over risk by counting empty bottles of alcohol vs non and checking in on the guest wobble factor.
- And as a plan B I could have emergency curry in the freezer to soak up the booze.

The Alien is managed and I don't need to get up at 4am or slave all day Christmas eve.

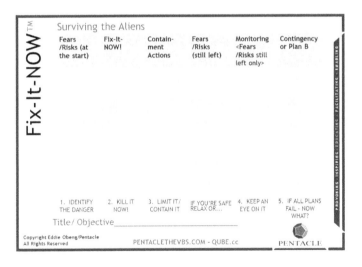

Fears /Risks (at the start)	Fix-It-NOW!	Containment Actions	Fears /Risks (still left)	Monitoring <Fears /Risks still left only>	Contingency or Plan B
1. IDENTIFY THE DANGER	2. KILL IT NOW!	3. LIMIT IT / CONTAIN IT	IF YOU'RE SAFE RELAX OR...	4. KEEP AN EYE ON IT	5. IF ALL PLANS FAIL - NOW WHAT?

Surviving the Aliens

Fix-It-NOW™

Title / Objective_____

Insight: What have you discovered? What are your big 'so what' aliens? Did you dig down to make sure there was a real 'so what?' that needed a solution? What will you do to kill them dead? Contain them? Monitor them? And what is your Plan B? How do you now feel about the change and making sure it stay's risk free?

 Reflection: When you plan things, you might have a tendency to think 'it will all be fine' and 'I'll deal with it later' and do nothing. Or you might panic about all the things that might go wrong, get in a tizz, and do nothing. But there is a third way. One that thinks about all the aliens (things that might eat us) and kills them dead before they can even become a thing that might eat us. It's called pre-elimination of risk. By working through the tool upfront and by coming up with actions to remove the alien before it's even spotted your space-ship you will make the changes in your life a whole lot easier to manage.

 **Points time:** 20 points for every alien that has a real 'so what?' 'eeek' moment.

10 points for each alien you kill dead, contain, monitor, or have a plan B for.

Collect an extra 20 points if you actually go and do the thing to kill it dead.

Health points = _____

So, how to kill those Christmas Aliens?

I think about the meal. While I like cooking, I'm not a fan of cooking a Christmas-type meal. I also hate shopping and supermarkets and realize that it could cost a lot. Combining these three things means I have a big 'so what?' alien. And that 'so what?' is that I'll get very stressed and grumpy, which could lead to me drinking too much, shouting at people, storming up to my room, or all of the above. This would not be ideal.

So, I think, I need to get all Sigourney Weaver on this thing.

Kill it dead: I create a menu that everyone can contribute to equally and which will be easy to put together quickly on the day. Shared cost, shared work, shared shopping.

Contain it: I get to pick what I'll prepare (so will enjoy the cooking bit) and if it goes wrong, we will take equal blame.

Monitor it: Check in regularly that everyone is on track with their task.

Plan B: I have soup and beef stew frozen in portions in the freezer for a rainy day that can be used if needed.

Take that, Sigourney Weaver.

My next alien is that everyone will keep interfering and causing unnecessary problems if they've been assigned tasks they're not happy with. I know, for example, those that normally host will find it difficult to take a back seat. And I can hardly give my cousin a cooking task when she has a six-hour drive beforehand.

So how might I kill this particular alien dead?

Easy. I pull out TeamFit™, a tool I often use for teams on projects and work out what type of change I have.[53] I know my outcome and goal (to have a jolly, happy, stress-free Christmas) but have never done this type of Christmas before so don't really know **how** to do it to ensure success. This means it's a Quest type of project.

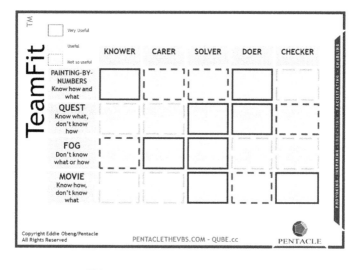

TeamFit™ tells me that for a Quest I need Solvers and Doers, followed by Carers and Knowers. I'm unlikely to need a checker.

---

[53] Remember I talked about these in life ninja moves 1, on page 48.

I don't have a choice of team (those attending) but I do know them well enough I think to make a fairly accurate guess as to which role they would fit.

I've devised the very clever menu and so I must be the Solver.[54] Why 'clever', you ask? Because it can all be either pre-prepared and/or takes 40 minutes to cook. Cold starters; 40-minute main course,[55] cheese plate. Microwave the Christmas pud and have a range of cold deserts. *Et voilà.*

There are two Doers in the mix, the ones who would normally host themselves. These get the more complicated bits of the menu. They have a lot of experience cooking and it will keep them busy in the week leading up to Christmas so I know they will do a good job.

There are two Carers in the crowd who want to do things because they care but aren't really sure what they can do. One I assign table decorations to, the other will make sure the dogs are happy and walked before dinner. These tasks can be as easy or complex as they like, but they care so they will do a good job.

I have two Knowers. Cheese and wine, I think. One to pair the wine with the menu, the other to create a nice mixed cheeseboard. They will both take the job seriously, likely providing tasting notes too and so I know they will do a good job.

---

[54] Clearly. I am solving the common Christmas challenges by murdering aliens. That is problem solving in a nutshell. This could be the new *Die Hard* Christmas/not Christmas movie franchise.

[55] Duck confit for the bird and ginger beer boiled ham that just needs 40 mins in the oven, in case you were wondering. You're welcome.

And finally, I have one Checker which isn't really needed but I ask them to set up the WhatsApp group and just, well, check in that things are going smoothly. I know they will take the role seriously and so I know they will do a good job.

Bob, from next door, didn't have anything to do. He charmed his way out of activity, so I let him off lightly.

Next, I need to solve the gift dilemma. I realize that even if I can think of a low cost gift idea it could still start to add up and cheap things tend to end up in the bin so it's all a bit wasteful. I'm mulling this over at breakfast, looking around the room for inspiration when I notice a cookbook I've put out for my neighbour to borrow. Books, I think. Perfect.

After breakfast I head into my nearest town which has a charity bookshop where all books are just £1. A knitting book, a Dilbert book, a Scottish poetry book, a tarot card book. I quickly find a book that I know each person will love, or at least find funny and appreciate. The books may well, I think, end up back in the shop at some point but it means everyone is a winner. It's cheap (for me), everyone gets a personal gift they'll appreciate, the charity shop wins at least once, and possibly twice, if the books are returned.

It's Christmas day morning. I wake up with my usual stretch before I remember it's Christmas day and that Santa (may) have been, and I get a tad excited. This could have been a home alone and slightly sad day for me. But by using my resources (tools and people) well, by noticing what my brain and body have been doing in relation to the stressors, traumas, and panic stations, I have, I think, managed to Change Ninja this year pretty well. The new chap disappears to let the dogs out[56] and make coffee while I lie in bed feeling like I really am in a Hollywood movie. This time last year, I think, I was looking forward to an OK day with the in-laws telling me the same old stories and starting to ponder an adventure. And an adventure I have had.

The new chap returns with a large mug of steaming coffee while trying to hide a Christmas stocking behind his back and not let the dogs get hold of it. Santa, it seems, really has been. We get up slowly, have a lovely long breakfast, take the dogs for a nice long walk before exchanging gifts. I start to clean up the wrapping paper when the doorbell goes. My cousin has arrived and after lots of hugs and happy Christmases I leave them to get settled and start to get the table ready for dinner later.

An hour or so later and guests start to arrive, I seem to be the hostess with the mostess, pouring drinks, introducing people to each other, letting those who brought food over sort it out, putting the oven on

---

[56] That 'must have' on my dating list has worked out well!

ready for the 40-minute menu and put the plates on the hotplate to warm up. Everything, and I mean everything is coming together as planned. Once we've had our buffet style starters, I ask everyone to take a seat so we can get the hot food out. Of course, everyone asks, 'where do you want me?' and of course I have already thought of this. On the table, along with all the decorations, crackers, and silly glasses are the book gifts, wrapped up and used as place settings. Ninja style!

We have a wee toast and tuck into the main course, followed by cheese (with tasting notes!) and desserts. Then there is another wee toast, for moi, for putting such a good day together. This could have been quite a stressful and expensive day I reflect. But it wasn't. Because I nail-gunned those aliens dead and it has really been a very easy, and extremely lovely day. I look over at the new chap and grin.

And that is how I Ninja'd Christmas!

Chapter 19

Making lemonade

I t's a few months later. April 19th to be exact.[57] It's exactly one year since I moved to the new life in the new house in the new location. A year ago today I was full of anxiety and fear about what this new life would hold and was emotionally broken and grief stricken about the life I no longer had. But I refused to give in, and found just enough resolve to move me forward, one tiny step at a time. I paid close attention to my body, my physical feelings, and the doubts running through my head. I knew that the brain wasn't always doing the best thing for me and so I learnt how to trick it to give me enough capacity to help me make the right decisions, however scary they felt, and however much I couldn't imagine a good outcome.

---

[57] That date again. It's a recurring 'good' date.

To recap, last January I was contemplating a move to the country with my lifelong partner. In February, after discovering something grim, I decided I had to be brave and end the relationship. In March, I sold my home of 20 years before buying a crazy house in the country that I moved to in April. In May, I decided to say yes to everything and in doing so made friends with people I perhaps would never have previously thought of as potential friends and done things I'd never previously imagined I'd do, such as loch 'douking'. June and July felt like being in a Hollywood romance as all the things I'd imagined about country living with rose tinted spectacles actually happened including getting a very cute new puppy.[58] August was crazy and saw me dealing with the emotions of the previous few months, realizing I might need to think about dating, publishing a book, going on a crazy camping trip with a couple of less than fun lasses and three dogs, trying out dating (and testing my boundaries) before meeting someone special. And then I Ninja'd Christmas.

It's exactly a year to the day since I moved to this new life, and I have just taken off in a plane from Morocco where I've spent 12 days travelling around on a fairly independent tour with my rucksack and new better half (who is snoring next to me as I write). We have explored cities and villages, climbed mountains, and swum in waterfalls, slept in swanky Riads and low-key homestays. I have played with wild (tame)

---

[58] Say 'hi' to Dougie.

monkeys, eaten tagines in every flavour, bought the requisite rug, and had the requisite hammam. Oh, and yesterday I was proposed to. Yes, that's right dear reader. A proposal of marriage. And of course. I had to say YES![59]

If someone had told me any of this last March, when I was all in a panic about having nowhere to live, I would have laughed in their face. It was utterly, utterly unimaginable. When people told me it would be fine, I didn't believe them, couldn't believe them. But I could, I knew, in the moment, choose how I responded to each and every doubt, panic, and indecision my brain created. I could create my own 'happily ever after' story even if I had no idea what that would look like. I hadn't even been able to imagine being happy again.

And that is my story, and how I *choose* to tell it.

---

[59] The wedding, at the time of writing, will take place on 18th April, exactly a year to the day since we became engaged, and exactly two years to the day since I left my old life behind. This means the 19th April starts yet another new and exciting episode in my life.

Chapter 20

Over to you

So, how you did you do at Ninjaing Life alongside me?

At the start of the book, you began this adventure with me. After the thing that happened, happened, our Life Score dropped to 0, our Health Score of 20 and we were fresh out of bottles of lemonade. Your aim was to finish the book with three full Lives, 100% Health and a Crate of Lemonade by using the tools as you went on some of your very own challenges. Not only did I want you to get some answers to your current challenges quickly, but I also wanted you to practise using the tools. Practice helps build new neural pathways, and the stronger the pathway becomes the more the thought process will become

automated.[60] And if the thought process of how to deal with *X* by doing *Y* is automated then next time something similar happens you will instinctively know what to do rather than your brain shouting 'run!' Your logic will stay switched on and you will work out the answer without too much of the 'eeek' of fear.

Let's add up your total points.

Chapter	Page	Points
Starting point		20
Into the abyss	53	
Between a rock and a hard place	70	
Plans that stick	88	
Decisions, decisions	99	
Magic box of tricks	112	
The fog begins to lift	125	
Endings and beginnings	141	
A Tinderella story	151	
Sami's fables	168	
Tell me that story again	176	
Ninjaing Christmas	186	
Total health points collected		

Now convert your score however you wish to use it.

---

[60] If you've ever learnt a musical instrument you will know that by practicing chords over and over you can now play them without thinking about it.

Health Points convert directly to your Health Score but each Life requires 100 Health points and each Bottle of Lemonade requires 50 Health points.

How did you do?

_____Lives   _____Health Score

_____Bottles of Lemonade (six per crate)

Now congratulate yourself. Well done you. You, like me, have taken a pounding, but by using your resources wisely, the life skills you have, the tools you know or have learnt, and the people you have in your network, you have managed to Change Ninja your life.

I'd like to share one final tool though. Because you can bet your behind this won't be the last time you have to manage big or unwanted or emotional change. This one final push will help you form some new habits. Habits that mean next time something happens, big or small, you will know *instantly* how to handle it, almost without thinking about it. This last tool and learning will mean you can Ninja at life again and again and again.

Life ninja move 12

Story: Remember the last time you decided you were going to do something on a regular basis, to form a new habit. It was possibly going for a walk every day before breakfast. Or having a lunch break everyday instead of sitting in back-to-back meetings. It might even have been trying to stop a bad habit like eating biscuits at 2pm every day when you realized you'd missed lunch.

Habits are hard to form because we forget to do them. But think about all the things you do that you don't even think about like cleaning your teeth or putting on your socks. You don't think about these things because there are strong neural pathways in your brain to do these automatically, without thinking. The brain likes these tasks because they use less energy and so they are brain 'friendly'. For new habits and behaviours, ones you do automatically, you therefore need to build some new pathways by doing the same thing enough times to become automatic. And here's how to do it.

Tool:[61] Follow these steps to create new habits.

1. Set a goal or outcome. What is it you want to achieve? An example might be 'I want to improve my

---
[61] BJ Fogg – *Tiny Habits*.

overall health and wellbeing by walking every day.'

2. Don't set yourself an initial goal of walking 10,000 steps every day. It's highly likely you will do this for three days, miss two days, and then give up.

3. Instead score your motivation levels (low to high). If it's low, you might want to change your goal. Habits are had to form even with high levels of motivation.

4. Then score how difficult the task is (low to high). This is useful for breaking it into manageable chunks.

5. Now choose a trigger point to remind you about the new behaviour you want to develop. Something you already do every day without thinking about and can use to trigger the new behaviour. 'When I switch on the kettle for breakfast', for example.

6. Choose a small, manageable activity to get you started. Walking for five minutes before morning coffee for example.

7. Write out the new habit, 'When I put the kettle of for breakfast, I will go for a five-minute walk before having my coffee'.

8. You now have a trigger for when to do the new behaviour (which makes it easier to remember to do) and even on the busiest of days you know you will have the time to do it because the action is manageable.

9. Decide how you will celebrate when you do the daily action. This is important as it tells your brain this is a good thing which increases the neural pathway growth which is needed to make this activity a habit. An extra large coffee could be a good shout.

10. Slowly increase the amount of time you walk for, setting new goals on a regular basis. Make sure they are manageable.

11. You also need to decide how you will celebrate once you have achieved the bigger goal of say going for a 30-minute walk every day. A new pair of trainers might just work.

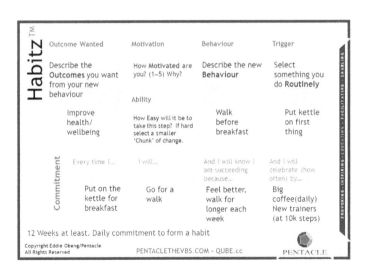

Habitz™	Outcome Wanted	Motivation	Behaviour	Trigger
	Describe the Outcomes you want from your new behaviour	How Motivated are you? (1–5) Why?	Describe the new Behaviour	Select something you do Routinely
		Ability		
	Improve health/ wellbeing	How Easy will it be to take this step? If hard select a smaller 'Chunk' of change.	Walk before breakfast	Put kettle on first thing
Commitment	Every time I...	I will...	And I will know I am succeeding because...	And I will celebrate (how often) by...
	Put on the kettle for breakfast	Go for a walk	Feel better, walk for longer each week	Big coffee(daily) New trainers (at 10k steps)

12 Weeks at least. Daily commitment to form a habit

Application: Think about how you are going to make some of the things you've learnt in this book become habit forming:

1. Set a goal with a clear outcome of what you want to do differently.
2. Determine how motivated you are (1–5). If it's very low then perhaps you don't plan to do anything different as a result of reading this book, which is, of course, perfectly fine!
3. Determine how hard or easy you think it will be help break the task into smaller chunks.
4. Decide on your small first step you can do that is manageable.
5. Identify a trigger of when you will do it.
6. Write out 'Whenever I (trigger) I will (action)'.
7. Decide how you will celebrate every time you do it.
8. Decide how you will celebrate when you've achieved your overall goal of becoming a Change Ninja.

Insight: Do you have a plan? Are you ready to build that new habit? Have you found a good trigger and is it manageable? More importantly how will you celebrate?

Write down on a sticky note '*Whenever I (trigger),
I will (new activity), and I will celebrate by...*'.

Put the sticky note somewhere you'll see it often.

 Reflection: New habits require not only
the goal but motivation, ability, and
triggers to be aligned to create the new
behaviour and is helped by celebrating
whenever you do it. After some time, you will find you
are doing the new habit without even thinking about
it. That is when you really should celebrate!

 **Points time:** Celebrate right now by giving
yourself whatever points you feel you
deserve. You are totally Ninjaing in life. You
deserve it.

Bonus health points_____

Chapter 21

Twelve rules for ninjaing life

1. Remember we are all the same in that we all have fears, worries, and doubts. We might fear and worry and doubt different things, but we also all have, somewhere, the same superpowers to find a way through them. You just need to remember to use your resources in the best possible way and try not to tackle everything head on.

2. Always celebrate the good things however small they might seem. Congratulate yourself. Often. Never be afraid to feel proud of what you've done. Never downplay or underplay your achievements or listen to others who downplay what you've done. You deserve better.

3. Trust your gut. It's mostly right. The gut is often referred to as the second brain. The subconscious fearful brain predicts what might happen next to try and save you from the unknown that might spell danger. That's a scientific fact. The gut has its own way of letting you know what feels right. I don't know if that's a scientific fact or not, but it *feels* right. So – you know – trust it.

4. Use the tools and the summary grid in Chapter 4 to jump straight to a tool when you have a challenge, any challenge, it doesn't need to be a life-changing one to use the tool. Use the tools and previous learning.

5. If you physically feel 'off' it's a warning sign. Don't ignore it. Try and work out where the problem is coming from, decide which of your resources is best for this particular problem and go do something about it. Ignore your physical feelings at your peril but do choose to ignore the (negative) emotional response that goes with it.

6. Always, always, do things in small chunks. Tiny steps if necessary. Tiny steps move you forward, give room for reward when they're done, motivate you to do the next task, and distract you from the scary stuff that keeps you awake at night.

7. Remember reality doesn't really care what you think. And doubts are only there to distract you.

It's easy to say, 'but it's too hard to do' and do nothing. It's easy to listen to the doubts and do nothing. Over thinking is just that, thinking. It doesn't change actual reality, but it does help you procrastinate. Remind yourself of this when all you feel able to do is think of the worst outcome and when the doubts are taking over. You will learn to start ignoring them, at least enough to allow you to move forward a small teeny tiny toatie wee step.

8. You only need to move forward one small, tiny step.

9. Reframing stories has a huge amount of power. And if you do it enough you can rewire you brain into new ways of thinking. You just need to find one tiny positive reference in your story. One tiny benefit. Even the most negative of things can often have a benefit.

10. Label your emotions, say them out loud, tell a story, write them down. If you name them the physical associated (bad) feeling will reduce. For example, if you say to someone 'I feel angry' you will notice the feeling of anger subsides a little.

11. Remember we can all choose, to some extent, how we tell a story. To others and yourself. Being vulnerable, telling your story the way you want to tell it makes the story real, it becomes your reality. It's like magic.

12. Practice, practice, practice. Even with these tools I sometimes wobbled a bit, well a lot. But the more you practise them the more they will be easy to pull out of the bag when you absolutely need them to get you back on the right path to move forward.

With these 12 Change Ninja Tales;

With these 12 Life Ninja Moves;

With these 12 Ninjaing Rules;

You too, can go forth and Change Ninja your life.

And remember… You should always, always, always celebrate!

References

Neuroscience

The Idiot Brain: A Neuroscientist Explains What Your Head Is Really Up To – Dean Burnett

How Emotions Are Made: The Secret Life of the Brain – Lisa Feldman Barrett

The Science of Stuck: Breaking Through Inertia to Find Your Path Forward – Britt Fran

Reframe Your Brain: The User Interface for Happiness and Success – Scott Adams

Derren Brown's bootcamp (Podcast)

Huberman Lab (Podcast)

Tools

David Rock (SCARF): https://davidrock.net/

Carol Dweck, Growth Mindset: www.mindsetworks.com/Science/Default

The coaching habit – Michael Bungay

Tiny Habits: The Small Changes That Change Everything – BJ Fog

All other tools provided are from Pentacle the Virtual Business School

Projects

Perfect Projects – Eddie Obeng

The Complete Leader – Eddie Obeng

All Change! – Eddie Obeng

Life change

Hagitude: Reimagining the Second Half of Life – Sharon Blackie

Devorgilla Days – Kathleen Hart

Want to know more?

Dr Tammy Watchorn:
tammy@change-ninja.com
www.change-ninja.com

Get in touch for:
Training – Becoming a Change Ninja
Residentials – The Ninja Way
Bespoke team events and training
Keynote Presentations
Or just for a natter

Acknowledgments

My wing people – in no particular order: Jacqueline Cooper, Harry Cooper, Joe Cooper, Robert Cooper, Emma Hogg, Eddie Obeng, Susan Ross, Suzanne Whyte, Jo Chapman, Vanessa Randle, Jo Stanford, Sam Brandes, Emily Walsh, Susan Burney, Lorna Jackson, Alex Barker, Donna Sawyers, Ani Kaprekar, David Girdler, and Lorna Jackson.

The loch douckers – Kelly, Donna, Jo, Wendy, Jen, Bobbie, Pam, Jean, Brenda, Colin, Steven, Colleen, Leanne, Christine, Dee, Susie, and Elly who welcomed me with open arms.

The new family, whether they like it or not – Jen and Paul, Jane, Bob and Gavin.

And some others who were part of the story albeit fleetingly. Duncan, Blairgowrie runners, BARI project, Flour, Shona, Fi, Iona, Cath, Lynn, Shara, Renyl, Alison, Annmarie, Joscelyn, Mike, Ian, and Anne R.

And a big thank you to the PIP team. You are rather lovely to work with.

Index

Note: references to footnotes show both the page number and the note number (45n27).

A quick word from Practical Inspiration Publishing...

We hope you found this book both practical and inspiring – that's what we aim for with every book we publish.

We publish titles on topics ranging from leadership, entrepreneurship, HR and marketing to self-development and wellbeing.

Find details of all our books at: www.practicalinspiration.com

 Did you know...

We can offer discounts on bulk sales of all our titles – ideal if you want to use them for training purposes, corporate giveaways or simply because you feel these ideas deserve to be shared with your network.

We can even produce bespoke versions of our books, for example with your organization's logo and/or a tailored foreword.

To discuss further, contact us on info@practicalinspiration.com.

 Got an idea for a business book?

We may be able to help. Find out more about publishing in partnership with us at: bit.ly/PIpublishing.

Follow us on social media...

 @PIPTalking

@pip_talking

@practicalinspiration

@piptalking

Practical Inspiration Publishing

Cut me out!

WINGMAN